AUDIT RISK ALERT

Understanding the Responsibilities of Auditors for Audits of Group Financial Statements

2013

12849-359

STRENGTHENING AUDIT INTEGRITY
SAFEGUARDING FINANCIAL REPORTING

Notice to Readers

This Audit Risk Alert (alert) is intended to help auditors understand and implement AU-C section 600, *Special Considerations—Audits of Group Financial Statements (Including the Work of Component Auditors)* (AICPA, *Professional Standards*), which supersedes Statement on Auditing Standards No. 1 section 543, *Part of Audit Performed by Other Independent Auditors* (AICPA, *Professional Standards*), and paragraphs .12–.13 of AU section 508, *Reports on Audited Financial Statements* (AICPA, *Professional Standards*). The purpose of this alert is to provide guidance on implementing AU-C section 600, which is an auditing standard established by the Auditing Standards Board (ASB). Accordingly, this alert does not address any auditing standards established by the Government Accountability Office, the Public Company Accounting Oversight Board, or any other auditing standard setting body. Auditors of group financial statements that are subject to the requirements of another auditing standard setting body (in lieu of or in addition to) those established by the ASB are encouraged to read those standards in conjunction with this alert.

This publication is an *other auditing publication*, as defined in AU-C section 200, *Overall Objectives of the Independent Auditor and the Conduct of an Audit in Accordance With Generally Accepted Auditing Standards* (AICPA, *Professional Standards*). Other auditing publications have no authoritative status; however, they may help the auditor understand and apply generally accepted auditing standards.

In applying the auditing guidance included in an other auditing publication, the auditor should, using professional judgment, assess the relevance and appropriateness of such guidance to the circumstances of the audit. The auditing guidance in this document has been reviewed by the AICPA Audit and Attest Standards staff and published by the AICPA and is presumed to be appropriate. This document has not been approved, disapproved, or otherwise acted on by a senior technical committee of the AICPA.

Recognition

Contributors and Reviewers

Jim Clous
Bob Dohrer
Jennifer Haskell
Ilene Kassman
Maria Manasses
Michael Westervelt

AICPA Staff

Christopher Cole
Technical Manager
Accounting and Auditing Publications

The AICPA gratefully appreciates the invaluable assistance Philip J. Santarelli provided in creating this publication.

Feedback

As you encounter audit or accounting issues that you believe warrant discussion in an alert, please feel free to share them with us. Any other comments that you have about the alert also would be appreciated. You may e-mail these comments to A&APublications@aicpa.org.

TABLE OF CONTENTS

Paragraph

What Are Group Audits?

.01 Group audits involve the audit of financial statements that include the financial information of more than one component (group financial statements). AU-C section 600, *Special Considerations—Audits of Group Financial Statements (Including the Work of Component Auditors)* (AICPA, *Professional Standards*), expands previous guidance related to using the work of other auditors to encompass audits of group financial statements. AU-C section 600 introduces a number of new terms, concepts, and requirements related to group audits that will significantly affect current practice (see paragraph .19 of this Audit Risk Alert [alert]). Because AU-C section 600 is much broader than previous guidance, it is important for auditors to fully understand the requirements therein. AU-C section 600 is effective for audits of group financial statements for periods ending on or after December 15, 2012.

.02 The following questions and answers point out some of the major changes in the new standard, which may assist auditors in recognizing when they are involved in an audit of group financial statements:

1. *What are group financial statements?* Group financial statements include the financial information of more than one component. The concept of group financial statements is broader than consolidated or combined financial statements because it encompasses business activities in addition to separate entities. Additionally, this standard applies in all audits of group financial statements regardless of whether different auditors are involved in the audit.

2. *What is a component?* A *component* is an entity or business activity for which group or component management prepares financial information that is required to be included in the group financial statements. A component may include, but is not limited to, subsidiaries, geographical locations, divisions, investments, products or services, functions, processes, or component units of state or local governments. Equity method investments are also components that are scoped into the standard. However, other investments using fair value measurements are generally not considered components.

3. *How are the previous concepts of* other auditor *and* principal auditor *changed in this standard?* The focus of the previous standard was the interaction between the auditors. AU-C section 600 changes that focus to the unique characteristics of a group reporting entity and how an auditor should obtain sufficient audit evidence to render an opinion on the group financial statements. An auditor who performs work on the financial statements, or financial information, of a component is now referred to as the *component auditor* rather than *an other auditor*. The *auditor of the group financial statements*, which encompasses the firm and group engagement team, including the group engagement partner, replaces the concept of the *principal auditor*. A member of the group engagement team may perform work on the financial information of a component for the group audit at the request of the group engagement team. When this is the case, such a member of the group engagement team is also a component auditor. Note that when the component is being audited by the group engagement team, the group engagement team is filling the role of the component auditor.

Although members of the group engagement team may be filling the role of a component auditor, typically this will not add any additional performance requirements to the group audit other than, in some circumstances, the need to apply component materiality.

4. *Do the requirements change for making reference to the work of other auditors?* AU-C section 600 better articulates the degree of involvement required when reference is made to the audit of component auditors in the auditor's report on the group financial statements. It establishes certain conditions that are necessary for the group engagement partner to make reference to a component auditor in the auditor's report on the group financial statements (see paragraph .111 of this alert for further discussion of these conditions). Moreover, AU-C section 600 clarifies that the group engagement partner is responsible for the opinion on the group financial statements, regardless of whether reference is made to component auditors. Additionally, AU-C section 600 establishes requirements that apply to all group audits regardless of whether reference is made to the work of the component auditor. These requirements expand the level of communication with the component auditors and the considerations of the group engagement partner when determining the acceptability of using the component auditor's work.

5. *Are there new procedures that are required when assuming responsibility for the work of other auditors?* Certain provisions of AU-C section 600 apply to all group audits regardless of whether reference is made to the audit of a component auditor in the auditor's report on the group financial statements. AU-C section 600 specifically articulates the procedures the group engagement team is required to perform when a component auditor is involved in the group audit. Additional specific procedures are applicable when the auditor of the group financial statements assumes responsibility for the work of a component auditor or is performing audit procedures on the components directly.

.03 This alert summarizes the new standard and provides implementation guidance for the auditor of the group financial statements. For component auditors, it also describes the specific matters that the group engagement team is required to communicate to the component auditor and to request that the component auditor also communicate with the group engagement team. However, auditors will need to read AU-C section 600, including its application material, in its entirety to fully understand its effect on current practice.

Organization of This Alert

.04 This alert is organized in the following major sections:

- *Introduction to the Clarified Statements on Auditing Standards.* Paragraphs .05–.20 of this alert provide an introduction to AU-C section 600 (paragraphs .05–.10 of this alert) that includes a discussion of the applicability (paragraphs .11–.17 of this alert) and objectives of AU-C section 600 (paragraph .18 of this alert), as well as definitions used in AU-C section 600 (paragraph .19 of this alert).

- *Overview of AU-C Section 600.* Paragraphs .21–.72 of this alert provide a detailed overview of AU-C section 600 using the same format as AU-C section 600. This section of the alert first presents a discussion of the group engagement team's responsibilities in all audits of group financial statements (paragraphs .22–.35 and .42–.56 of this alert), as well as the requirements applicable when the auditor of the group financial statements does not assume responsibility for, and makes reference to, the work of a component auditor (paragraphs .36–.41 of this alert). It then provides a discussion of the additional requirements in an audit of group financial statements when the auditor of the group financial statements assumes responsibility (that is, he or she does not make reference to the work of the component auditor in the auditor's report on the group financial statements) for the work of a component auditor (paragraphs .57–.72 of this alert).

- *How AU-C Section 600 Will Affect Practice.* Paragraphs .72–.161 of this alert first provide an overview of how specific sections of AU-C section 600 will generally affect audits of group financial statements (paragraphs .72–.103 of this alert) and then detail specific areas that will generally require additional consideration in the application of AU-C section 600 (paragraphs .104–.146 of this alert). This section of the alert also discusses considerations specific to audits of state and local governmental entities (paragraphs .147–.161 of this alert).

- *Resource Central.* Paragraphs .162–.172 of this alert provide a variety of resources to assist the auditor in understanding and implementing the new standards. Also found in this section are selected resources the auditor might find helpful in any financial statement audit and information on how these resources may be obtained or accessed.

- *Appendixes.* This alert contains five appendixes that include

  - answers to commonly asked questions related to the applicability and scope of AU-C section 600 issued by the AICPA as *Technical Practice Aids* (paragraph .173 of this alert);

  - a decision-making flowchart related to components included in AU-C section 600 (paragraph .174 of this alert);

  - two examples, one for a not-for-profit organization and one for a local government, related to applying group materiality and group performance materiality[1] to components (paragraph .175 of this alert);

  - four different examples involving various aspects of AU-C section 600 (paragraph .176 of this alert); and

  - additional resources the auditor may access online (paragraph .177 of this alert).

---

[1] *Materiality* and *performance materiality* are defined in AU-C section 320, *Materiality in Planning and Performing an Audit* (AICPA, *Professional Standards*).

Introduction to the Clarified Statements on Auditing Standards

.05 The Auditing Standards Board (ASB) has substantially completed its Clarity Project to clarify existing generally accepted auditing standards (GAAS) to make them easier to read, understand, and apply. Statement on Auditing Standards (SAS) Nos. 117–127 have been issued in the clarity format and supersede all prior SASs except SAS No. 65, *The Auditor's Consideration of the Internal Audit Function in an Audit of Financial Statements* (AICPA, *Professional Standards*, AU sec. 322 and AU-C sec. 610).[2]

.06 The clarified SASs articulate more clearly the objectives of the auditor and the requirements with which the auditor has to comply when conducting an audit in accordance with GAAS. SAS No. 122, *Statements on Auditing Standards: Clarification and Recodification* (AICPA, *Professional Standards*), was issued in October 2011 and contains AU-C section numbers instead of AU section numbers. AU-C is a temporary identifier to avoid confusion with references to existing AU sections, which remain effective through 2013, in AICPA *Professional Standards*. The AU-C identifier will revert to AU in 2014, by which time SAS No. 122 becomes effective for all engagements performed in accordance with GAAS. SAS No. 122 recodifies the AU section numbers as designated by SAS Nos. 1–121 based on equivalent International Standards on Auditing (ISA) numbers. AU-C section numbers for clarified SASs with no equivalent ISAs have been assigned new numbers. SAS No. 122 applies to audits of financial statements, including group financial statements, for periods ending on or after December 15, 2012.

.07 AU-C section 600 supersedes AU section 543, *Part of Audit Performed by Other Independent Auditors* (AICPA, *Professional Standards*), and paragraphs .12–.13 of AU section 508, *Reports on Audited Financial Statements* (AICPA, *Professional Standards*).

.08 SAS No. 127, *Omnibus Statement on Auditing Standards—2013* (AICPA, *Professional Standards*), was subsequently issued in January 2013 and, among other matters, amends AU-C section 600. These amendments relate to making reference to component auditors and are discussed further in paragraph .29 of this alert.

.09 AU section 543, written in 1972, primarily provided guidance for the auditor in deciding (*a*) whether to serve as the principal auditor and use the work of other auditors and (*b*) the form and content of the principal auditor's report in those circumstances. AU-C section 600 is more broadly focused on how to conduct an effective audit of group financial statements. In addition to the requirements of GAAS established in other SASs that are applied in audits of group financial statements (including but not limited to the risk assessment standards), it addresses special considerations that apply to group audits, in particular those that involve component auditors. Additionally, AU-C section 600 specifically articulates the procedures the group engagement team is required to perform when a component auditor is involved in the group audit. It also better articulates the degree of involvement required when reference is

---

[2] Proposed Statement on Auditing Standards (SAS), *Using the Work of Internal Auditors*, which supersedes SAS No. 65, *The Auditor's Consideration of the Internal Audit Function in an Audit of Financial Statements* (AICPA, *Professional Standards*, AU sec. 322 and AU-C sec. 610), was issued for exposure on April 15, 2013, with a comment period ending on July 15, 2013.

made to component auditors in the auditor's report on the group financial statements.

.10 The requirements of AU-C section 600 that may have the most impact on current practice include, but are not limited to, the following areas:

- Acceptance and continuance considerations
- The group engagement team's process to assess risk, including specific considerations affecting group financial statements
- The determination of materiality to be used to audit the group financial statements, including the materiality to be used for procedures related to components
- Exercising professional judgment in identifying components
- Identification of significant components and the related audit procedures to be performed
- Communications between the group engagement team and component auditors
- Assessing the adequacy and appropriateness of audit evidence by the group engagement team in forming an opinion on the group financial statements
- Consideration of factors when determining whether to make reference to the work of the component auditor(s)

Applicability of AU-C Section 600

.11 Paragraphs .01–.08 of AU-C section 600 broadly discuss responsibilities and requirements of the group engagement partner, the group engagement team, and the firm. In AU-C section 600, requirements to be undertaken by the group engagement partner are addressed to the group engagement partner. When the group engagement team may assist the group engagement partner in fulfilling a requirement, the requirement is addressed to the group engagement team. When it may be appropriate in the circumstances for the firm to fulfill a requirement, the requirement is addressed to the auditor of the group financial statements.

.12 AU-C section 600 applies to audits of group financial statements and addresses special considerations that apply to group audits, in particular those that involve component auditors. Accordingly, a critical aspect of this section is the identification of the components that are included in the group financial statements. Another important aspect is whether reference will be made to the audit of a component auditor in the auditor's report on the group financial statements. The requirements in paragraphs .51–.65 of AU-C section 600 are applicable to all components except those for which the auditor of the group financial statements is making reference to the work of a component auditor. All other requirements of AU-C section 600 apply regardless of whether the auditor of the group financial statements is assuming responsibility for the work of component auditors.

.13 An auditor may find AU-C section 600 useful, adapted as necessary in the circumstances, when he or she involves other auditors in the audit of financial statements that are not group financial statements. For example, in an audit of the financial statements of a single entity that does not prepare consolidated financial statements, an auditor may involve another auditor to observe the inventory count or inspect physical fixed assets at a remote location. In such situations, an auditor may adapt the guidance in AU-C section 600 with respect to obtaining an understanding of the other auditor's professional competence, communicating the work to be performed, or being involved in the work of the other auditor.

.14 The requirements of AU-C section 220, *Quality Control for an Engagement Conducted in Accordance With Generally Accepted Auditing Standards* (AICPA, *Professional Standards*), apply regardless of whether the group engagement team or a component auditor performs the work on the financial statements of a component. Certain requirements of AU-C section 220 are applicable to the group engagement partner. For example, the group engagement partner is required to be satisfied that those performing the group audit engagement, including component auditors, collectively possess the appropriate competence and capabilities. In addition, the group engagement partner is responsible for the direction, supervision, and performance of the group audit engagement. The group engagement partner is also responsible for deciding, individually for each component, to either

- assume responsibility for, and thus be required to be involved in, the work of a component auditor, insofar as that work relates to the expression of an opinion on the group financial statements, or
- not assume responsibility for the work of a component auditor and, accordingly, make reference to the audit of a component auditor in the auditor's report on the group financial statements.

.15 AU-C section 600 assists the group engagement partner in meeting the requirements of AU-C section 220 when component auditors perform work on the financial information of components.

.16 In a group audit, detection risk includes the risk that (*a*) a component auditor may not detect a misstatement in the financial information of a component that could cause a material misstatement of the group financial statements and (*b*) the group engagement team may not detect this misstatement. When the group engagement partner decides to assume responsibility for the work of a component auditor, AU-C section 600 explains the matters that the group engagement team considers when determining the nature, timing, and extent of its involvement in the risk assessment procedures and further audit procedures performed by component auditors on the financial information of the components. The purpose of this involvement is to obtain sufficient appropriate audit evidence on which to base the audit opinion on the group financial statements.

.17 This alert provides an overview of the requirements of AU-C section 600 and provides guidance for applying those requirements in the audit of group financial statements. Among other information, AU-C section 600 provides the following information and examples (not included in this alert) that the group engagement team may find helpful:

- Illustrations of auditor's reports on group financial statements (exhibit A, "Illustrations of Auditor's Reports on Group Financial Statements")
- Examples of component auditor confirmations related to a group audit of the financial statements (exhibit B, "Illustrative Component Auditor's Confirmation Letter")

- Examples of matters about which the group team obtains an understanding in the audit of group financial statements (appendix A, "Understanding the Group, Its Components, and Their Environments—Examples of Matters About Which the Group Engagement Team Obtains an Understanding")

- Examples of conditions or events that may indicate risks of material misstatement of the group financial statements (appendix B, "Examples of Conditions or Events That May Indicate Risks of Material Misstatement of the Group Financial Statements")

- Required and additional matters the group engagement team may include in its letter of instruction (appendix C, "Required and Additional Matters Included in the Group Engagement Team's Letter of Instruction")

Objectives of AU-C Section 600

.18 The objectives of the auditor as delineated in paragraph .10 of AU-C section 600 are to determine whether to act as the auditor of the group financial statements and, if so, to

- determine whether to make reference to the audit of a component auditor in the auditor's report on the group financial statements;

- communicate clearly with component auditors; and

- obtain sufficient appropriate audit evidence regarding the financial information of the components and the consolidation process to express an opinion about whether the group financial statements are prepared, in all material respects, in accordance with the applicable financial reporting framework.

Definitions

.19 Paragraphs .11–.12 of AU-C section 600 define the following terms for purposes of GAAS:

> **component.** An entity or business activity for which group or component management prepares financial information that is required by the applicable financial reporting framework to be included in the group financial statements.

> **component auditor.** An auditor who performs work on the financial information of a component that will be used as audit evidence for the group audit. A component auditor may be part of the group engagement partner's firm, a network firm of the group engagement partner's firm, or another firm.

> **component management.** Management responsible for preparing the financial information of a component.

> **component materiality.** The materiality for a component determined by the group engagement team for the purposes of the group audit.

> **group.** All the components whose financial information is included in the group financial statements. A group always has more than one component.

> **group audit.** The audit of group financial statements.

group audit opinion. The audit opinion on the group financial statements.

group engagement partner. The partner or other person in the firm who is responsible for the group audit engagement and its performance and for the auditor's report on the group financial statements that is issued on behalf of the firm. When joint auditors conduct the group audit, the joint engagement partners and their engagement teams collectively constitute the group engagement partner and the group engagement team. AU-C section 600 does not, however, deal with the relationship between joint auditors or the work that one joint auditor performs in relation to the work of the other joint auditor. (*Group engagement partner* and *firm* refer to their governmental equivalents when relevant).

group engagement team. Partners, including the group engagement partner, and staff who establish the overall group audit strategy, communicate with component auditors, perform work on the consolidation process, and evaluate the conclusions drawn from the audit evidence as the basis for forming an opinion on the group financial statements.

group financial statements. Financial statements that include the financial information of more than one component. The term *group financial statements* also refers to combined financial statements aggregating the financial information prepared by components that are under common control.

group management. Management responsible for the preparation and fair presentation of the group financial statements.

group-wide controls. Controls designed, implemented, and maintained by group management over group financial reporting.

significant component. A component identified by the group engagement team (i) that is of individual financial significance to the group or (ii) that, due to its specific nature or circumstances, is likely to include significant risks of material misstatement of the group financial statements.

.20 Reference to *the applicable financial reporting framework* means the financial reporting framework that applies to the group financial statements. Reference to *the consolidation process* includes the following:

- The recognition, measurement, presentation, and disclosure of the financial information of the components in the group financial statements by way of inclusion, consolidation, proportionate consolidation, or the equity or cost methods of accounting

- The aggregation in combined financial statements of the financial information of components that are under common control

Overview of AU-C Section 600

.21 AU-C section 600 provides guidance for when the auditor of the group financial statements assumes responsibility for the work of a component auditor and when the auditor does not assume responsibility for the work of a component auditor (that is, the group auditor makes reference to the audit of the component auditor in the auditor's report on the group financial statements). An audit of group financial statements involves establishing an overall group audit strategy and group audit plan (including identifying the components and the extent to which the group engagement team will use the work of component auditors). The decision whether the auditor's report on the group financial statements will make reference to the audit of a component auditor should be made by the group engagement partner. When the auditor of the group financial statements assumes responsibility for the work of a component auditor, no reference is made to the component auditor in the auditor's report on the group financial statements. Alternatively, when the auditor of group financial statements does not assume responsibility for the work of a component auditor, the auditor will make reference to the audit of the component auditor in the auditor's report on the group financial statements. Reference in the auditor's report on the group financial statements to the fact that part of the audit was conducted by a component auditor is not to be construed as a qualification of the opinion. Rather, such reference is intended to communicate

1. that the auditor of the group financial statements is not assuming responsibility for the work of the component auditor and

2. the source of the audit evidence with respect to those components for which reference to the audit of component auditors is made.

Whether reference is made to the component auditor does not change the objective of the auditor to "obtain sufficient appropriate audit evidence regarding the financial information of the components and the consolidation process to express an opinion about whether the group financial statements are prepared, in all material respects, in accordance with the applicable financial reporting framework" (paragraph .10 of AU-C section 600).

Responsibilities of the Group Engagement Team

.22 Paragraph .13 of AU-C section 600 states that the group engagement partner is responsible for the direction, supervision, and performance of the group audit engagement in compliance with professional standards, applicable regulatory and legal requirements, and the firm's policies and procedures. In addition, the group engagement partner is responsible for determining whether the auditor's report that is issued is appropriate in the circumstances.

Acceptance and Continuance

.23 Paragraphs .14–.17 of AU-C section 600 provide that the group engagement partner should determine whether sufficient appropriate audit evidence can reasonably be expected to be obtained regarding the consolidation process and the financial information of the components on which to base the group audit opinion. The group engagement partner should evaluate whether the group engagement team will be able to obtain sufficient appropriate audit evidence, either through the (a) work of the group engagement team or (b) through the use of the work of component auditors, to act as the auditor of the group financial statements and to report as such on the group financial statements. However, the auditor's report on the group financial statements should not make reference to a component auditor unless the conditions discussed in paragraphs .29–.30 of this alert are met. In addition, the auditor of the group financial statements is required in accordance with AU-C section 210, *Terms of*

Engagement (AICPA, *Professional Standards*), to agree upon the terms of the group audit engagement with management or those responsible for governance as appropriate.

.24 Restrictions imposed by group management may lead the group engagement partner to conclude that it will not be possible for the group engagement team to obtain sufficient appropriate audit evidence through the work of the group engagement team or through use of the work of the component auditors. If the possible effect of this inability will result in a disclaimer of opinion on the group financial statements, due to a scope limitation, the auditor of the group financial statements should

- not accept the engagement in the case of a new engagement;
- withdraw from the engagement if it is a continuing engagement (when possible under applicable law or regulation); or
- when the entity is required by law or regulation to have an audit, disclaim an opinion on the group financial statements after having performed the audit of the group financial statements to the extent possible.

Overall Audit Strategy and Audit Plan and Understanding the Group, Its Components, and Their Environments

.25 Paragraphs .18–.21 of AU-C section 600 require the group engagement team to

- establish an overall group audit strategy and to develop a group audit plan, which should be reviewed and approved by the group engagement partner;
- enhance its understanding of the group, its components, and their environments (including group-wide controls) obtained during the acceptance and continuance stage; and
- obtain an understanding of the consolidation process, including the instructions issued by group management to components.

.26 When establishing an overall group audit plan, AU-C section 600 also requires the group engagement team to assess the extent to which the group engagement team will use the work of component auditors and whether the auditor's report on the group financial statements will make reference to the audit of a component auditor. The understanding obtained by the group engagement team should be sufficient to (*a*) confirm or revise its initial identification of components that are likely to be significant and (*b*) assess the risks of material misstatement of the group financial statements, whether due to fraud or error.

Understanding a Component Auditor

.27 Regardless of whether reference will be made to the audit of a component auditor in the auditor's report on the group financial statements, paragraphs .22–.23 of AU-C section 600 place certain requirements on the group engagement team with respect to the component auditor. AU-C section 600 provides that in all audits of group financial statements, the group engagement team should obtain an understanding of the following:

- Whether a component auditor understands and will comply with the ethical requirements that are relevant to the group audit and, in particular, is independent[3]
- A component auditor's professional competence[4]
- The extent, if any, to which the group engagement team will be able to be involved in the work of the component auditor
- Whether the group engagement team will be able to obtain information affecting the consolidation process from a component auditor
- Whether a component auditor operates in a regulatory environment that actively oversees auditors

.28 The group engagement team should obtain sufficient appropriate audit evidence relating to the financial information of a component without making reference to the audit of that component auditor in the auditor's report on the group financial statements or otherwise using the work of the component auditor when

- a component auditor does not meet the independence requirements that are relevant to the group audit or
- the group engagement team has serious concerns about whether a component auditor understands and will comply with the ethical requirements, including independence, that are relevant to the group audit or about a component auditor's professional competence.

Determining Whether to Make Reference to a Component Auditor in the Auditor's Report on the Group Financial Statements

.29 Paragraphs .24–.27 of AU-C section 600 state that it is the group engagement partner's responsibility to decide whether to make reference to a component auditor in the auditor's report on the group financial statements. If the group engagement partner decides not to make reference to the component auditor in the auditor's report on the group financial statements, the group engagement team is required to be involved in the work of the component auditor. The auditor's report on the group financial statements should not make reference to a component auditor unless (a) the group engagement partner has determined that the component auditor has performed an audit of the financial

---

[3] When such standards are applicable to the group audit, the group engagement team is also required to determine that a component auditor is independent under *Government Auditing Standards* issued by the Comptroller General of the United States of the U.S. Government Accountability Office.

As discussed in paragraph .A46 of AU-C section 600, *Special Considerations—Audits of Group Financial Statements (Including the Work of Component Auditors)* (AICPA, *Professional Standards*), when the component auditor is not subject to the AICPA Code of Professional Conduct, compliance by the component auditor with the ethics and independence requirements set forth in the International Federation of Accountants Code of Ethics for Professional Accountants is sufficient to fulfill the component auditor's ethical responsibilities in the group audit.

[4] The group engagement team is also required to evaluate a component auditor's professional competence. Information for United States auditors can be obtained through the peer review system as well as the state societies or state boards of accountancy. For auditors in foreign jurisdictions, information may be obtained from the Public Company Accounting Oversight Board inspection process, through the professional organizations in the foreign jurisdiction, or through inquiry with global associations or networks with which the firm may be associated.

statements of the component in accordance with the relevant requirements of GAAS and (b) the component auditor has issued an auditor's report that is not restricted as to use.[5]

.30 When a component auditor has performed an audit of the component financial statements in accordance with auditing standards other than GAAS or, if applicable, auditing standards promulgated by the Public Company Accounting Oversight Board (PCAOB), the group engagement partner may evaluate, using professional judgment, whether such audit meets the relevant requirements of GAAS. For example, audits performed in accordance with ISA promulgated by the International Auditing and Assurance Standards Board (IAASB) are more likely to meet the relevant requirements of GAAS than audits performed in accordance with auditing standards promulgated by bodies other than the IAASB. The relevant requirements of GAAS are those that pertain to planning and performing the audit of the component financial statements and do not include those related to the form of the auditor's report. Additional guidance is provided in paragraph .A53 of AU-C section 600.

When Component Financial Statements are Prepared Under a Different Financial Reporting Framework

.31 If the component auditor reports on financial statements prepared in accordance with a different financial reporting framework than the group financial statements, there are two additional requirements in paragraph .26 of AU-C section 600 to be addressed before the group engagement partner can make reference to the component auditors' report. The first requirement is that the measurement, recognition, presentation, and disclosure criteria that are applicable to all material items in the component's financial statements under the financial reporting framework used by the component are similar to the criteria that are applicable to all material items in the group's financial statements under the financial reporting framework used by the group.

.32 There are several considerations when the group engagement partner is concluding on whether the relevant financial reporting framework is similar to the group's financial reporting framework. The greater the number of differences or the greater the significance of the differences between the criteria used for measurement, recognition, presentation, and disclosure of all material items in the component's financial statements under the financial reporting framework used by the component and the financial reporting framework used by the group, the less similar they are.

.33 Financial statements prepared and presented in accordance with International Financial Reporting Standards (IFRSs) and International Financial Reporting Standard for Small and Medium-sized Entities, as issued by the International Accounting Standards Board, are generally viewed as more similar to financial statements prepared and presented in accordance with accounting principles generally accepted in the United States of America (GAAP) than financial statements prepared and presented in accordance with jurisdiction-specific reporting frameworks or adaptations of IFRSs. In most cases, special

---

[5] SAS No. 125, *Alert That Restricts the Use of the Auditor's Written Communication* (AICPA, *Professional Standards*, AU-C sec. 905), was issued in December 2011 and is effective for audits of financial statements for periods ending on or after December 15, 2012. The standard addresses the auditor's responsibility when required, or when the auditor decides, to include language that restricts the use of the auditor's written communication (audit report or other written communication) in a generally accepted auditing standards engagement.

purpose frameworks set forth in AU-C section 800, *Special Considerations— Audits of Financial Statements Prepared in Accordance With Special Purpose Frameworks* (AICPA, *Professional Standards*), are not similar to GAAP.

.34 The second requirement is that the group engagement team has obtained sufficient appropriate audit evidence for purposes of evaluating the appropriateness of the adjustments to convert the component's financial statements to the financial reporting framework used by the group without the need to assume responsibility for, and thus be involved in, the work of the component auditor.

.35 Evaluating whether the financial statements of the component have been appropriately adjusted to conform with the financial reporting framework used by the group is based on a depth of understanding of the component's financial statements that ordinarily is not obtained unless the auditor of the group financial statements assumes responsibility for, and thus is involved in, the work of the component auditor. In rare circumstances, however, the group engagement partner may conclude that the group engagement team can reasonably expect to obtain sufficient appropriate audit evidence for purposes of evaluating the appropriateness of the adjustments to convert the component's financial statements to the financial reporting framework used by the group without the need to assume responsibility for, and thus be involved in, the work of the component auditor.

Making Reference to a Component Auditor in the Auditor's Report on the Group Financial Statements

.36 When the group engagement partner decides to make reference to the audit of a component auditor in the auditor's report on the group financial statements, paragraph .28 of AU-C section 600 states that the group engagement team should obtain sufficient appropriate audit evidence with regard to such components by

- performing the procedures required under AU-C section 600, except for those that are only applicable when assuming responsibility for the work of a component auditor (that is, not making reference to the work of the component auditor in the auditor's report on the group financial statements), and

- reading the component's financial statements and the component auditor's report thereon to identify significant findings and issues and, when considered necessary, communicating with the component auditor in that regard.

.37 Paragraphs .29–.31 of AU-C section 600 state that if the group engagement partner decides to make reference to the audit of a component auditor, the auditor's report on the group financial statements should clearly indicate that the component was not audited by the auditor of the group financial statements but audited by the component auditor. The auditor's report on the group financial statements should clearly indicate the magnitude of the portion of the financial statements audited by the component auditor. If the group engagement partner decides to name a component auditor in the auditor's report on the group financial statements, (*a*) the component auditor's express permission should be obtained and (*b*) the component auditor's report should be presented with that of the auditor's report on the group financial statements.

.38 If the component auditor reported on component financial statements prepared in accordance with a different financial reporting framework, there are reporting requirements related to the auditor's report on the group financial statements. These include disclosing the following in the auditor's report on the group financial statements:

- The financial reporting framework used by the component
- That the auditor of the group financial statements is taking responsibility for evaluating the appropriateness of the adjustments to convert the component's financial statements to the financial reporting framework used by the group

.39 If the component auditor did not report that he or she conducted the audit in accordance with GAAS or PCAOB standards, and the component auditor performed additional audit procedures in order to meet the relevant requirements of GAAS, then the report on the group financial statements should also include

- the auditing standards used by the component auditor and
- that additional audit procedures were performed by the component auditor to meet the relevant audit requirements of GAAS.[6]

.40 Other factors for the group engagement partner's consideration in the decision whether to make reference to component auditors' reports on financial statements prepared in accordance with a different financial reporting framework include

- effectiveness of group-wide controls over the consolidation process, in particular the reconciliation to the group financial reporting framework.
- the understanding that the group engagement team has with respect to the other financial reporting framework, especially where there are complex transactions to evaluate.
- the understanding of the component and its operating environment.
- the ability of the group engagement team to obtain sufficient information to enable auditing the reconciliation to the group financial reporting framework.
- access to other professionals that have the expertise to advise the group engagement team with respect to the other financial reporting framework and required adjustments.

.41 When the component auditor has modified his or her opinion or has included an emphasis-of-matter or other-matter paragraph in his or her report, the auditor of the group financial statements should determine the effect this may have on the auditor's report on the group financial statements. When appropriate, the auditor of the group financial statements should modify the opinion on the group financial statements or include an emphasis-of-matter or other-matter paragraph in his or her report on the group financial statements.

---

[6] Exhibit A, "Illustrations of Auditor's Reports on Group Financial Statements," of AU-C section 600 provides examples of audit reports when making reference to component auditors reporting on financial statements prepared in accordance with a different financial reporting framework or conducting audits in accordance with different audit standards.

Materiality

.42 In the context of a group audit, materiality is established for the group financial statements as a whole and component materiality is established for those components (1) on which the group engagement team will perform an audit or a review or (2) for which the auditor of the group financial statements will assume responsibility for the work of a component auditor who performs an audit or a review. Different materiality may be established for different components, and the aggregate of component materiality may exceed group materiality. Component materiality should be determined taking into account all components, regardless of whether reference is made to the audit of the component auditor in the auditor's report on the group financial statements. Paragraph .51 of AU-C section 600 provides additional requirements related to materiality that apply when the auditor of the group financial statements assumes responsibility for the work of a component auditor (see paragraph .57 of this alert).

.43 Determining materiality is the responsibility of the group engagement team, and AU-C section 600 establishes requirements for the determination of materiality that are applicable to all audits of group financial statements. In all group audits, the following should be determined by the group engagement team:

- Materiality, including performance materiality, for the group financial statements as a whole when establishing the overall group audit strategy
- Materiality for particular classes of transactions, account balances, or disclosures in the group financial statements when, in the specific circumstances of the group, material misstatements of lesser amounts than materiality for the group financial statements as a whole could reasonably be expected to influence the economic decisions of the users taken on the basis of the group financial statements
- Component materiality for those components on which the group engagement will perform an audit or review or for which the auditor of the group financial statements will assume responsibility for the work of a component auditor who performs an audit or review
- The threshold above which misstatements cannot be regarded as clearly trivial to the group financial statements

.44 With respect to component materiality, as mentioned in the preceding list, the group engagement team should determine it by taking into account all components, regardless of whether reference is made to the audit of a component auditor in the auditor's report on the group financial statements. In a situation in which reference is being made to a component auditor's report, there is no requirement for the group auditor to communicate the apportioned component materiality to the component auditor. However, it may be helpful for the group auditor to understand the level at which the component auditor performed its procedures because the materiality assigned to such components may affect the materiality available for the rest of the components. To reduce the risk that the aggregate of uncorrected and undetected misstatements in the group financial statements exceed the materiality for the group financial statements as a whole, component materiality should be lower than the materiality for the group financial statements as a whole. However, the aggregate component materiality may, and is likely to, exceed group materiality. Component performance materiality should be lower than performance materiality for the group financial statements as a whole and may be determined by the group engagement team or the component auditor. Accordingly, when assuming responsibility for the component auditor's work, the group engagement team is required to evaluate the appropriateness of performance materiality at the component level.

Responding to Assessed Risks

.45 Appropriate responses to assessed risks of material misstatement for some or all account balances or classes of transactions may be implemented at the group level without involving the component auditor. Paragraph .33 of AU-C section 600 establishes requirements for the group engagement team to respond to the assessed risks of material misstatement that are applicable to all audits of group financial statements. In addition, paragraphs .52–.58 of AU-C section 600 provide additional requirements in this area that apply when the auditor of the group financial statements assumes responsibility for the work of a component auditor.

.46 The group engagement team should test, or have a component auditor test on the group engagement team's behalf, the operating effectiveness of group-wide controls over the consolidation process or the financial information of components when

- the auditor wishes to place reliance on the controls over the consolidation process rather than applying substantive audit procedures or

- substantive procedures alone cannot provide sufficient appropriate audit evidence at the assertion level.

Consolidation Process

.47 As used in AU-C section 600, the *consolidation process* refers to both

1. recognition, measurement, presentation, and disclosure of financial information of components in the group financial statements through inclusion, consolidation, proportionate consolidation, or the equity or cost methods of accounting and

2. aggregation in combined financial statements of financial information of components under common control.

.48 The consolidation process may require adjustments to amounts reported in the group financial statements that do not pass through the usual transaction processing systems and, therefore, may not be subject to the same internal controls as other financial information. With respect to the consolidation process, paragraphs .34–.39 of AU-C section 600 provide that the group engagement team should

- obtain an understanding of group-wide controls and the consolidation process, including the instructions issued by group management to components.

- test, or request that the component auditor test, the operating effectiveness of group-wide controls if the nature, timing, and extent of the work to be performed on the consolidation process are based on an expectation that group-wide controls are operating effectively or when substantive procedures alone cannot provide sufficient appropriate audit evidence at the assertion level.

- design and perform further audit procedures to respond to the assessed risks of material misstatement of the group financial statements arising from the consolidation process, including evaluating whether all components have been included in the group financial statements.
- evaluate the appropriateness, completeness, and accuracy of consolidation adjustments and reclassifications and evaluate whether any fraud risk factors or indicators of possible management bias exist.
- evaluate whether the financial information of a component that has not been prepared in accordance with the same accounting policies applied to the group financial statements has been appropriately adjusted for purposes of preparing and fairly presenting the group financial statements.
- determine whether the financial information identified in a component auditor's communication is the financial information that is incorporated in the group financial statements.
- evaluate whether appropriate adjustments have been made to the financial statements of any component (in accordance with the applicable financial reporting framework) with a financial reporting period-end that differs from that of the group.

Subsequent Events

.49 Recognition or disclosure of subsequent events affecting the group financial statements is the responsibility of group management and likewise the responsibility of component management in the component financial statements. However, paragraph .40 of AU-C section 600 requires the group engagement team, or the component auditors performing audits on financial information of components, to perform procedures related to subsequent events affecting components. Specifically, the group engagement team or the component auditors should perform procedures designed to identify events at components that occur between the dates of the financial information of the component and the date of the auditor's report on the group financial statements that may require adjustment to, or disclosure in, the group financial statements. Paragraph .59 of AU-C section 600 provides additional requirements related to subsequent events that apply when the auditor of the group financial statements assumes responsibility for the work of a component auditor.

Communication With a Component Auditor

.50 Paragraphs .41–.42 of AU-C section 600 require certain communications between the group engagement team and the component auditor in all group audits (discussed subsequently) and additional communications when the auditor of the group financial statements assumes responsibility for the work of a component auditor (see paragraphs .67–.68 of this alert). The group engagement team should communicate its requirements to a component auditor on a timely basis. This communication should include the following:

1. A request that the component auditor, knowing the context in which the group engagement team will use the work of the component auditor, confirm that the component auditor will cooperate with the group engagement team.

2. The ethical requirements relevant to the group audit and, in particular, the independence requirements.

3. A list of related parties prepared by group management and any other related parties of which the group engagement team is aware. (The group engagement team should request the component auditor to communicate on a timely basis related parties not previously identified by either group management or the group engagement team. Additionally, the group engagement team should identify such additional related parties to other component auditors.)

4. Identified significant risks of material misstatement of the group financial statements, due to fraud or error, that are relevant to the work of the component auditor.

.51 In addition, the group engagement team should request a component auditor to communicate matters relevant to the group engagement team's conclusion with regard to the group audit. This communication should include the following:

1. Whether the component auditor has complied with ethical requirements relevant to the group audit, including independence and professional competence

2. Identification of the financial information of the component on which the component auditor is reporting

3. The component auditor's overall findings, conclusions, or opinion

Evaluating the Sufficiency and Appropriateness of Audit Evidence Obtained

.52 When the group engagement team concludes that sufficient appropriate audit evidence has not been obtained on which to base the group audit opinion, the group engagement team may (a) request a component auditor to perform additional procedures or (b) perform its own procedures on the financial information of the component. Paragraphs .43–.45 of AU-C section 600 include requirements for the group engagement team and the group engagement partner with respect to evaluating the sufficiency and appropriateness of the audit evidence obtained by the group engagement team and the component auditor. In addition, AU-C section 600 provides additional requirements in this area (see paragraph .69 of this alert) that apply when the auditor of the group financial statements assumes responsibility for the work of a component auditor.

.53 The group engagement team should evaluate the component auditor's communication and discuss significant findings and issues identified as a result of that evaluation with the component auditor, component management, or group management, as appropriate. In addition, the group engagement team should evaluate whether sufficient appropriate audit evidence has been obtained from (a) the audit procedures performed on the consolidation process and (b) work performed by the group engagement team and the component auditors on the financial information of the components on which to base the group audit opinion. The group engagement partner should evaluate the effect on the group audit opinion of any

●   uncorrected misstatements either identified by the group engagement team or communicated by the component auditor and

- instances in which there has been an inability to obtain sufficient appropriate audit evidence.

Communication With Group Management and Those Charged With Governance of the Group

.54 Certain communications with group management and those charged with governance of the group are required by paragraphs .46–.49 of AU-C section 600 in all group audits (discussed subsequently) with additional communications required when the auditor of the group financial statements assumes responsibility for the work of a component auditor (see paragraph .71 of this alert). With respect to communications with group management and those charged with governance of the group, the group engagement team should do the following:

1. Communicate material weaknesses and significant deficiencies in internal control that are relevant to the group.

2. Communicate any fraud identified by the group engagement team or brought to its attention by the component auditor or information indicating a fraud may exist on a timely basis to the appropriate level of group management.

3. When a component auditor has been engaged to express an audit opinion on the financial statements of a component, request group management to inform component management of any matter of which the group engagement team becomes aware that may be significant to the financial statements of the component but of which component management may be unaware.

4. Discuss the matter with those charged with governance of the group if group management refuses to communicate matters in item 3 to component management. When the matters noted in item 3 remain unresolved, consider, subject to legal and professional confidentiality considerations, whether to

    a. advise the component auditor not to issue the auditor's report on the financial statements of the component until the matters are resolved or

    b. withdraw from the engagement.

.55 The group engagement team should communicate the following matters to those charged with governance of the group (in addition to any other matters required to be communicated by AU-C section 260, *The Auditor's Communication With Those Charged With Governance* [AICPA, *Professional Standards*], and any other relevant AU-C sections):

- An overview of the type of work to be performed on the financial information of the components, including the basis for the decision to make reference to the audit of a component auditor in the auditor's report on the group financial statements

- An overview of the nature of the group engagement team's planned involvement in the work to be performed by the component auditors on significant components

- Instances in which the group engagement team's evaluation of the work of a component auditor gave rise to concern about the quality of that auditor's work

- Any limitations on the group audit
- Fraud or suspected fraud involving group management, component management, employees who have significant roles in group-wide controls, or others in which a material misstatement of the group financial statements has or may have resulted from fraud

Documentation

.56 Paragraph .50 of AU-C section 600 requires documentation of certain matters in all group audits (discussed subsequently) as well as additional documentation requirements when the auditor of the group financial statements assumes responsibility for the work of a component auditor (see paragraph .72 of this alert). The following matters should be documented by the group engagement team:

- An analysis of components indicating those that are significant and the type of work performed on the financial information of the components.
- Written communications between the group engagement team and the component auditors about the group engagement team's requirements.
- Those components for which reference to the reports of component auditors was made in the auditor's report on the group financial statements.
- For those components for which reference is made in the auditor's report on the group financial statements to the audit of a component auditor,
  — the financial statements of the component and the report of the component auditor thereon.
  — when the component auditor did not conduct the audit in accordance with GAAS or PCAOB standards, the basis for the group engagement partner's determination that the component auditor's work met the relevant requirements of GAAS.

Additional Requirements Applicable When Assuming Responsibility for the Work of a Component Auditor

---

Help Desk: Information discussed in the following paragraphs applies only when the group engagement partner decides to assume responsibility and, therefore, not make reference to a component auditor in the auditor's report on the group financial statements. These requirements are in addition to those previously discussed that are applicable in all audits of group financial statements.

Materiality

.57 Paragraph .51 of AU-C section 600 states that the group engagement team should evaluate the appropriateness of performance materiality at the component level when assuming responsibility for the component auditor's work. AU-C section 320, *Materiality in Planning and Performing an Audit*

(AICPA, *Professional Standards*), provides guidance on determining performance materiality for purposes of assessing the risks of material misstatement and to design further audit procedures in response to assessed risks. Like component materiality, component performance materiality should be lower than performance materiality for the group financial statements as a whole.

.58 In some situations, the component auditor will be issuing a separate report to meet a legal or regulatory requirement in a different jurisdiction. In such cases, it may be beneficial for the group engagement partner to obtain information on the materiality and performance materiality that the component auditor intends to use. Often this may be lower than what the group engagement partner would have allocated to a particular component. In those cases, the lower materiality may be used and the group engagement partner may consider this lower materiality when determining component materiality for other components, which may be higher, and bearing in mind that individual component materiality is less than group materiality.

Determining the Type of Work to Be Performed on the Financial Information of Components

.59 For components for which the group engagement partner decides to assume responsibility for the work of component auditors, paragraph .52 of AU-C section 600 states that the group engagement team should determine the

- type of work to be performed by the group engagement team or by component auditors on its behalf on the financial information of the components and

- nature, timing, and extent of its involvement in the work of component auditors.

.60 In order to plan the work to be performed with respect to components for which the group engagement partner decides to assume responsibility, it is first necessary to identify which of those components are significant components (those that are individually financially significant or likely to include significant risks of material misstatement of the group financial statements). The following paragraphs discuss the group engagement team's responsibilities with respect to both significant components and those that are not significant. Appendix B, "Decision-Making Flowchart," of this alert provides steps that auditors might find helpful when applying the requirements of AU-C section 600 related to components.

Significant Components

.61 For components that are significant due to their individual financial significance to the group, paragraphs .53–.54 of AU-C section 600 state that the group engagement team, or a component auditor on its behalf, should perform an audit of the financial information of the component (adapted as necessary to meet the needs of the group engagement team) using component materiality. For components that are significant because they are likely to include significant risks of material misstatement of the group financial statements due to their specific nature or circumstances, the group engagement team, or a component auditor on its behalf, should perform one of more of the following:

- An audit of the financial information of the component (adapted as necessary to meet the needs of the group engagement team) using component materiality

- An audit of one or more account balances, classes of transactions, or disclosures relating to the likely significant risks of material misstatement of the group financial statements (adapted as necessary to meet the needs of the group engagement team)

- Specified audit procedures relating to the likely significant risks of material misstatement of the group financial statements

.62 When the group engagement team is considering the types of procedures to perform and instructions for the component auditor, guidance found in AU-C section 805, *Special Considerations—Audits of Single Financial Statements and Specific Elements, Accounts, or Items of a Financial Statement* (AICPA, *Professional Standards*), may be helpful even if that section is not applicable to the specific engagement. Also, there is no requirement for the component auditor to issue a report on the procedures when the group auditor is assuming responsibility for the component auditor's work. The component auditor's communication with the group engagement team may take the form of a memorandum of work performed or a more formal auditor's report, adapted as necessary to meet the needs of the group engagement team. Alternatively, the group engagement team can review the component auditor's working papers to obtain sufficient understanding of the procedures performed in order to conclude on the sufficiency of the evidence obtained.

Components That Are Not Significant Components

.63 For components that are not significant components, paragraphs .55–.56 of AU-C section 600 state that the group engagement team should perform analytical procedures at the group level. When the group engagement team determines that sufficient appropriate audit evidence on which to base the group audit opinion will not be obtained from certain procedures[7] specified in AU-C section 600, the group engagement team should select additional components that are not significant (varying, over time, which individual components are selected, which will introduce unpredictability into the audit process), and perform (or request a component auditor to perform) one or more of the following:

- An audit of the financial information of the component (adapted as necessary to meet the needs of the group engagement team) using component materiality

- An audit of one or more account balances, classes of transactions, or disclosures (adapted as necessary to meet the needs of the group engagement team)

- A review of the financial information of the component (adapted as necessary to meet the needs of the group engagement team) using component materiality

- Specified audit procedures

In situations in which there are a number of other than significant components, the group engagement team may determine the types of procedures performed

---

[7] Specifically identified procedures are (1) work performed on the financial information of significant components, (2) work performed on group-wide controls and the consolidation process, and (3) analytical procedures performed at the group level.

on different components over time. In doing so, an element of unpredictability can be brought into the process.

Involvement in the Work Performed by Component Auditors

.64 When a component auditor performs an audit or other specified audit procedures of the financial information of a significant component for which the auditor of the group financial statements is assuming responsibility for the component auditor's work, paragraphs .57–.58 of AU-C section 600 specify that the group engagement team should be involved in the risk assessment of the component to identify significant risks of material misstatement of the group financial statements. The nature, timing, and extent of this involvement are affected by the group engagement team's understanding of the component auditor but at a minimum should include the following:

- Discussing the component's business activities that are of significance to the group with the component auditor or component management
- Discussing the susceptibility of the component to material misstatement of the financial information due to fraud or error with the component auditor
- Reviewing the component auditor's documentation of identified significant risks of material misstatement of the group financial statements

.65 Significant risks of material misstatement of the group financial statements may be identified in a component for which the auditor of the group financial statements is assuming responsibility for the work of the component auditor. In such circumstances, the group engagement team should evaluate the appropriateness of the further audit procedures to be performed in response to such identified risks. Additionally, the group engagement team should determine whether it is necessary to be involved in the further audit procedures (based on its understanding of the component auditor). This involvement can take a variety of forms, such as reviewing relevant parts of the component auditor's audit documentation or requesting responses to specific inquiries relevant to the component entity.

Subsequent Events

.66 Recognition or disclosure of subsequent events affecting the group financial statements is the responsibility of group management and likewise the responsibility of component management in the component financial statements. When component auditors perform work other than audits of the financial information of components at the request of the group engagement team, paragraph .59 of AU-C section 600 requires the group engagement team to request the component auditors to notify the group engagement team if they become aware of events at those components that occur between the dates of the financial information of the components and the date of the auditor's report on the group financial statements that may require an adjustment to, or disclosure in, the group financial statements.

Communication With a Component Auditor

.67 When the auditor of group financial statements is assuming responsibility for the work of a component auditor, paragraphs .60–.61 of AU-C section 600 state that the communication should set out the work to be performed and the form and content of the component auditor's communication with the group engagement team. In the case of an audit or review of the financial information of the component, component materiality (and the amount[s] lower than the materiality for particular classes of transactions, account balances, or disclosures, if applicable) and the threshold above which misstatements cannot be regarded as clearly trivial to the group financial statements should also be included.

.68 The communication requested from the component auditor should contain additional communications when the auditor of the group financial statement is assuming responsibility for the work of a component auditor, including

- whether the component auditor has complied with the group engagement team's requirements.
- information on instances of noncompliance with laws or regulations at the component or group level that could give rise to material misstatement of the group financial statements.
- significant risks of material misstatement of the group financial statements, due to fraud or error, identified by the component auditor in the component and the component auditor's responses to such risks. The group engagement team should request the component auditor to communicate such significant risks on a timely basis.
- a list of corrected and uncorrected misstatements of the financial information of the component (misstatements below the threshold for clearly trivial misstatement need not be included).
- indicators of possible management bias regarding accounting estimates and application of accounting principles.
- a description of any identified material weaknesses and significant deficiencies in internal control at the component level.
- other significant findings and issues the component auditor communicated or expects to communicate to those charged with governance of the component, including fraud or suspected fraud involving
  — component management or employees having significant roles in internal control at the component level and
  — others that resulted in a material misstatement of the financial information of the component.
- any other matters that may be relevant to the group audit or that the component auditor wishes to draw to the attention of the group engagement team. This includes exceptions noted in the written representations that the component auditor requested from component management.

A group auditor may find it helpful to develop a standard instruction memorandum that can be tailored to the circumstances of each component.

Evaluating a Component Auditor's Communication and Adequacy of His or Her Work

.69 In accordance with paragraphs .62–.63 of AU-C section 600, the group engagement team should determine, based on the evaluation that the group engagement team is required by paragraph .43 of AU-C section 600 to make of a component auditor's communication, whether it is necessary to review other relevant parts of a component auditor's audit documentation. If the group engagement team concludes that the work of a component auditor is insufficient, the group engagement team should determine additional procedures to be performed and whether such procedures are to be performed by the component auditor or the group engagement team.

.70 The timeliness and quality of the communications with the component auditor are critical factors in enabling the group engagement team to conclude on the sufficiency of the component auditors' work. Communicating early in the engagement provides the ability for the group engagement team to request additional procedures or to perform additional procedures on their own.

Communication With Group Management and Those Charged With Governance of the Group

.71 Paragraph .64 of AU-C section 600 states that the group engagement team should determine which material weaknesses and significant deficiencies in internal control that component auditors have brought to the attention of the group engagement team should be communicated to group management and those charged with governance of the group.

Documentation

.72 Paragraph .65 of AU-C section 600 states that the group engagement team should include in the audit documentation the nature, timing, and extent of the group engagement team's involvement in the work performed by the component auditors on significant components, including, when applicable, the group engagement team's review of relevant parts of the component auditors' audit documentation and conclusions thereon.

How AU-C Section 600 Will Affect Practice

> **Help Desk**: The following paragraphs discuss, in general terms, how the requirements of AU-C section 600 affect audits of group financial statements. Paragraphs .73–.103 of this alert provide insights about how specific aspects of AU-C section 600 will generally affect audits of group financial statements. Specific considerations in the application of AU-C section 600 to all types of entities are discussed in paragraphs .104–.146 of this alert.

.73 Some auditors may not be significantly affected by the requirements of AU-C section 600 because they performed many of the required procedures on audit engagements prior to the implementation of this standard.

.74 It is important for the auditor to remember that the requirements of AU-C section 600 apply to all audits of group financial statements, which by definition are financial statements that include the financial information of more than one component. The requirements of AU-C section 600 related to materiality, consolidation, and selection of components and account balances for testing, for example, apply in all group audits regardless of whether the audit of a component auditor is referenced in the auditor's report on the group financial statements, or whether the group engagement team is performing audit procedures on the component directly without the involvement of other component auditors.

.75 If an auditor performs work on the financial information of a component that will be used as audit evidence for the group audit, that auditor is a component auditor. If an auditor performs work on the financial information of a component that will not be used as audit evidence for the group audit, that auditor is not considered a component auditor. For example, a subsidiary may require a statutory audit. If this subsidiary is insignificant to the group and the group engagement team decides that it is able to obtain sufficient appropriate audit evidence by performing analytical procedures at the group level and, therefore, does not plan to use the statutory audit work as audit evidence relating to the group's financial statements, the auditor performing the statutory audit is not considered a component auditor. Note that in such situations, it is not necessary to apply component materiality to such a component.

.76 AU-C section 600 makes a number of changes to previous practice related to auditing group financial statements, for example, when component auditors are involved in (a) auditing the entities included in the reporting entity or (b) performing audit procedures on any specified element, account, or item of a financial statement (such as a division, agency, or location). The changes to previous practice made by AU-C section 600 include not only nomenclature (see paragraph .19 of this alert) and new audit procedures, including additional communications between the group engagement team and component auditor(s), but also include additional requirements for the auditor of the group financial statements.

.77 These additional requirements require the group engagement team to gain an understanding of the internal control over the consolidation process or combination of the components into the group financial statements; assess the specific risks of material misstatement due to fraud or error related to the group; determine group materiality, including, as necessary, an assessment of group materiality at lower levels for specific account balances, classes of transactions (for instance, intercompany transactions), or disclosures; and determine component materiality when audit or review procedures are to be performed by the group engagement team or by component auditors for which the auditor of the group financial statements will assume responsibility for the component auditor's work.

General Practice Considerations

.78 The objectives of AU-C section 600 are to determine whether to act as the auditor of the group financial statements, and, if so, to (a) determine whether to make reference to the audit of a component auditor in the auditor's report on the group financial statements; (b) communicate clearly with component auditors; and (c) obtain sufficient appropriate evidence regarding the financial information of the components and the consolidation process to express an opinion about whether the group financial statements are prepared, in all material respects, in accordance with the applicable financial reporting framework.

.79 In many cases, component auditors may be from the same firm, or network of firms, as the auditor of the group financial statements. This may significantly affect how some firms plan and conduct audits of group financial statements. Similarly, management and those charged with governance of the group may also be management and those charged with governance of a component. At other times, the component auditor and the auditor of the group financial statements may be different firms, or management and those charged with governance of the group may be different from management and those charged with governance of a component. Implementing the requirements of AU-C section 600 may necessitate changes to firms' audit methodologies and quality control systems. For audits of group financial statements for periods ending on or after December 15, 2012, the audit strategy and audit plan of the group and component auditor will need to incorporate the requirements of AU-C section 600.

.80 Auditors may decide, but are not required, to modify the contents of the engagement letter and management representation letter for the requirements of AU-C section 600. For example, the group engagement partner might decide to include a section in the engagement letter noting the possible consequences if sufficient appropriate evidence cannot be obtained due to restrictions imposed by group management. Similarly, the group engagement partner may decide that additional representations from management might be necessary with respect to certain subsequent events at components that occur between the dates of the financial information of the components and the date of the auditor's report on the group financial statements. Additional guidance with regard to the engagement letter and management representation letter is provided, when applicable, in the following paragraphs.

.81 Because AU-C section 600 is part of the ASB's Clarity Project, some auditors may not be aware of the changes made to the requirements for audits of group financial statements. When a component auditor and the auditor of the group financial statements are not the same firm, the component auditor may not be aware of the requirements of AU-C section 600 until approached by the group engagement team. Likewise, the group engagement team may not be aware of the requirements until approached by a component auditor. As discussed in the following sections of this alert, there will be a number of changes in how group audits are performed under AU-C section 600. The majority of the changes directly affect the group engagement team, but there are direct and indirect effects on the component auditor as well. Auditors that expect to be auditors of group financial statements or component auditors involved in the audit of group financial statements may find it helpful to reach out to each other as soon as possible.

Help Desk: A thorough understanding of AU-C section 600 and timely communication between the group engagement team and the component auditor regarding its requirements will help ensure a smooth transition from the prior standards to the requirements of AU-C section 600.

.82 Management and those charged with governance of the group or component may not yet be aware of the changes in audits of group financial statements as a result of AU-C section 600. The group engagement partner (or the group engagement team) and the component auditor may discuss, as soon as possible, the requirements of AU-C section 600 and the resulting changes in the planned scope and timing of the audit of the group financial statements. Explanations of the additional work that may be required, including the additional involvement in the work of component auditors, may be particularly important when components are identified as significant components based on their individual financial significance to the group. In these circumstances, AU-C section 600 requires the group engagement team, or a component auditor on its behalf, to perform an audit of the financial information of the component (adapted as necessary to meet the needs of the group engagement team) using component materiality.

.83 In addition, it may be helpful to explain components in the context of audits of group financial statements to component or group management and those charged with governance. This may be particularly important in those engagements when components identified by the group engagement team for purposes of the group financial statements differ from those considered components by group or component management for operating or financial reporting purposes. For example, the group engagement team may identify a specific location as a component because it uses a different information processing system than the other business activities included in the group financial statements. Group management may identify its business activities by line of business rather than locations with differing systems.

.84 As noted elsewhere in this alert, the group engagement team and the component auditor (when the component auditor is another firm) may include items in the engagement letter or management representation letter related to their respective responsibilities under AU-C section 600.

.85 The following are examples of items that, at the discretion of the auditor of the group financial statements, may be included in the engagement letter or items in previous engagement letters that may be modified or expanded:

- Changes in language to include the terms *group* and *component* when appropriate.
- Management of the group's responsibility to select and apply an appropriate financial reporting framework for the group.
- The group engagement team's responsibilities with respect to identifying components (including significant components) for purposes of the group financial statements.
- Overview of the type of work to be performed on the financial information of the components, including the basis for the decision to make reference to the audit of a component auditor in the auditor's report on the group financial statements.
- Clarification of the reporting responsibilities of the group engagement team and any component auditors to which reference is expected to be made in the auditor's report on the group financial statements.
- Overview of the nature of the group engagement team's planned involvement in the work to be performed by the component auditors on the financial information of significant components.
- Responsibilities of the group engagement team with respect to testing of group-wide controls.
- Matters regarding the instructions related to the consolidation process that may be issued by group management to components.
- Expected communications between the group engagement team and group management and those charged with governance of the group, as appropriate, related to any
  - material weaknesses or significant deficiencies in internal control.

— fraud identified by the engagement team or brought to its attention by the component auditor or information indicating a fraud may exist.

— fraud or suspected fraud involving group management, component management, employees having significant roles in group-wide controls, or others in which a material misstatement of the group financial statements has or may have resulted from fraud.

— instances in which the group engagement team's evaluation of the work of a component auditor gave rise to a concern about the quality of that auditor's work.

— any limitations on the group audit (that is, access to information is restricted).

.86 Relevant management representations, or modifications to previous representations by management, may include, at the discretion of the auditor of the group financial statements, the following items:

- Changes in language in certain management representations to include the terms *group* and *component* when appropriate

- Acceptance of responsibility by group management or component management, as applicable in the circumstances, for preparing component financial information

- The copy of group management's instructions related to the consolidation process provided to the group engagement team represents the actual instructions issued to components

- Group and component management representations related to the consideration of subsequent events through the date of the group financial statements at the group and component levels

.87 AU-C section 600 uses the terms *financial information* and *component auditor*, which are broader in concept than the respective terms *financial statements* and *other auditors* that were found in prior standards. In addition, the term *component* is specifically defined and can encompass more than the subsidiaries, divisions, branches, components, or investments referenced in prior standards with respect to the work of other auditors. The term *component* is used differently in AU section 543 than it is in AU-C section 600. The broader concepts and more specific definitions in AU-C section 600 may affect the group audit strategy, group audit plan, or both, thereby resulting in fewer or more audit procedures performed by either the group engagement team or component auditor.

Determining Components

.88 In order to apply the requirements of AU-C section 600, it will be necessary for the group engagement team to identify the components that prepare financial information that is required, by the applicable financial reporting framework, to be included in the group financial statements. By definition, *components* are entities or business activities for which group or component management prepares financial information for inclusion in the group financial statements. The group engagement team obtains an understanding of the group, its components, and their environments that is sufficient to identify components that are likely to be significant components. Based on this, the group engagement team may conclude that the financial information included in the group financial statements can be effectively audited in aggregate rather than as separate components. Also, see paragraphs .152–.158 of this alert for further discussion of this requirement and practice issue as it relates to the audits of state and local governmental entities.

.89 The group engagement team obtains an understanding of the structure of the group financial reporting system as part of the risk assessment procedures when gaining an understanding of the entity and its environment. This may necessitate that the group engagement team enhance its understanding of the group, its components, and their environments, including group-wide controls. The group engagement team is required to obtain an understanding of the consolidation process, including instructions issued by group management to component management.

.90 The group engagement team is required to identify components that are likely to be significant components. To that end, the group engagement team may find it helpful to consider the following questions when identifying components:

- Does group management aggregate information from other entities or business activities to be included in the group financial statements? If so, is the information aggregated by

    — a parent and one or more subsidiaries, joint ventures, or investees accounted for by the equity method)?

    — a head office, one or more divisions or branches, or both?

    — function, process, product, or service?

    — groups of products or services or geographical locations?

- How does group management aggregate this information?

- Do the entities or business activities that are aggregated for the group financial statements use a common financial reporting system or separate systems?

- What controls are in place to reduce the risk that errors might occur in the aggregation process and not be detected or corrected in the group financial statements?

- What controls are in place at the separate entity or business activity level to reduce the risk that errors might occur and not be detected or corrected in the financial information that is aggregated in the group financial statements?

- Do the group financial statements include an investment accounted for under the equity method of accounting?

.91 Determining components (parent, subsidiaries, variable interest entities, component units of state or local governmental entities, and so on) that are included in the group financial statements will not likely present a major challenge for the group engagement team in a continuing engagement. However, the entity may be involved with certain entities or activities that are less obvious indicators of a component, including special purpose entities involved with nonprofit organizations, joint ventures, investments accounted for using the equity method of accounting,[8] employee retirement systems included in the component or group financial statements of state or local governments, investments in real estate investment trusts, and others. The auditor in a continuing engagement is typically aware of these other entities and should determine if they represent significant components for purposes of the group financial statements and document this decision process.

.92 Note that investments that are required to be reported at fair value normally would not be considered a component for purposes of AU-C section 600. For instance, investments in entities that are marked to fair value using the practical expedient provided in Financial Accounting Standards Board (FASB) *Accounting Standards Codification* (ASC) 820-10-35 would not be subject to the group audit procedures. Guidance for these circumstances can be found in AU-C section 501, *Audit Evidence—Specific Considerations for Selected Items* (AICPA, *Professional Standards*).

Help Desk: The auditor may need to make additional inquiries of group management with respect to related entities and parties to conclude that all components are included in the group financial statements.

.93 Determining if a specific business activity represents a component for purposes of AU-C section 600 requires professional judgment. If an entity's financial reporting system organizes financial information by function, product or service, or geographical location for purposes of external financial reporting, such functions, products or services, or locations may represent components for purposes of AU-C section 600. For example, group management may use financial information for several locations that is aggregated using a separate system or process from that used to prepare the group financial statements. The group engagement team may identify the locations as components. When financial information about a function, product or service, or geographical location is first part of the group's financial reporting system and then disaggregated by group management for operating purposes, the group engagement team may consider such financial information in whole or part as a class of transactions rather than components.

.94 Financial information classified by business activity for the group financial statements may represent the operations of a single legal entity or a number of legal entities. In such cases, the group engagement team may determine the component to be the business activity rather than the separate legal entities generating the activity. For example, the consolidated statement of comprehensive income may separately present revenues for major lines of business when revenues are generated by various subsidiaries. In this example, if the subsidiaries operate using similar systems or have similar controls, the group engagement team may identify the components as the lines of business rather than the subsidiaries that generated the revenues. If all other information on the consolidated statement of comprehensive income is presented at a group level, the group engagement team is not precluded from identifying the

---

[8] Paragraph .A2 of AU-C section 600 states that investments accounted for under the equity method constitute a component, and investments accounted for under the cost method may be considered components when the work and reports of other auditors constitute a major element of evidence for such investments. See appendix A, "Questions and Answers," of this alert for questions and answers related to equity method investments.

individual legal entities as components for purposes of performing the audit of the group financial statements.

.95 Group or component management may identify components for accounting purposes, operating purposes, or both and aggregate the related financial information differently for decision making purposes and for reporting in the group financial statements. It is the responsibility of group or component management, not the group engagement team, to identify and aggregate financial information that is required to be included in the group financial statements. The group engagement team may consider the type, quantity, and quality of the information available at these levels when identifying components for purposes of applying the requirements of AU-C section 600.

Determination of Significant Components

.96 After identifying the components in the audit of group financial statements, the group engagement team is required to determine if any of these components represent significant components. The group engagement team makes this determination based on whether the component is (*a*) of individual financial significance of the group or (*b*) likely to include significant risks of material misstatement (due to its specific nature or circumstances) of the group financial statements. Under the requirements of AU-C section 600, the group engagement team may identify entities or business activities as components or significant components that were not subject to audit procedures at that level in previous engagements under the prior standards. This may be the case in the audits of some state or local governmental entities that report pension and other post-retirement benefit plans in their fiduciary fund statements or in audits of entities that report equity method investments.

Components That Are Significant Components

> **Help Desk**: The group engagement team may determine that it is necessary to perform an audit (adapted as necessary to meet the needs of the group engagement team) of the financial information of one or more significant components. This may result in the group engagement team spending more time performing risk assessment or further audit procedures than in prior audits.

.97 Paragraphs .A6–.A8 of AU-C section 600 discuss ways the group engagement team may identify components that are individually financially significant. For example, applying a percentage to a chosen benchmark, such as group assets, liabilities, cash flows, revenues, expenditures, or net income, is described as a way to determine components that are individually financially significant. However, the group engagement team may determine that other methods or benchmarks are more appropriate based on the type of group entity as well as the specific facts and circumstances. For example, in audits of governmental entities, appropriate quantitative benchmarks for identifying significant components might include net costs or total budget. Qualitative considerations in audits of governmental entities may involve matters of heightened public sensitivity, such as national security issues, donor funded projects, or reporting tax revenue. Regardless of the type of group entity, the benchmarks or percentages used may change from one year to the next based on general or specific economic or operating conditions.

> **Help Desk**: A benchmark based on a percentage of assets may be different in the group audit of a not-for-profit organization than it is in the audit of a private sector entity. Likewise, net income may not be an appropriate benchmark to determine components that are financially significant to the group financial statements in the group audit of a government, not-for-profit organization, or employee benefit plan.

.98 It may be more difficult for the group engagement team to identify components that include risks of material misstatement that are significant to the group financial statements based on their specific nature or surrounding circumstances. Components with complex transactions from a business or accounting perspective may be identified as specific significant risks by the group engagement team. Such transactions might be those involving multiple or related parties, fair value measurements and disclosures, foreign currency, derivatives, alternative investments, and the like. In addition, a component might be considered significant (because it is likely to include significant risks of material misstatement) if it operates, for example, in a regulatory environment, if its business activities involve highly technical goods or services, or if it transacts business with a government entity that is subject to public records laws. For such significant components, AU-C section 600 allows the group engagement team to audit, or request a component auditor to audit, (adapted as necessary to meet the needs of the group engagement team) one or more account balances, classes of transactions, disclosures, or a combination of these in lieu of an audit of the component's financial information. The group engagement team may decide that this approach provides sufficient appropriate evidence to address specific significant risks that may be present in a component.

Audit Entities With Multiple Locations and Auditors With Multiple Offices

> **Help Desk**: AU-C section 600 may require audit firms auditing group financial statements of entities having multiple locations or audit firms having two or more offices involved in the audit of group financial statements to consider a number of factors in the group audit that may not have previously been considered.

.99 Requirements of AU-C section 600 may result in changes in determining the scope of audits of entities with multiple locations because the definition of a *component* encompasses not only entities but also business activities, which may be conducted at different locations. The audit of a single entity with multiple locations would not necessarily meet the definition of a *group audit* because the auditor may not consider the locations to be components. For example, a single corporate entity may own three coin-operated laundromats, each of them considered a division of the corporate entity. However, the transactions for all are maintained on one general ledger system, and all internal control over financial reporting is applied in the same manner to each location. In addition, none of the separate locations prepares financial information. In this situation, it is likely that the auditor may conclude that the locations are not *components* as defined in AU-C section 600.

.100 Additionally, AU-C section 600 may result in changes to the audit strategy or audit plan of group financial statements when a component auditor is part of the group engagement partner's firm.

Components That Are Not Significant Components

.101 When no component is identified as significant, it is possible that appropriate responses to assessed risks of material misstatement for some or all accounts or classes of transactions may be implemented at the group level, without the involvement of component auditors.

.102 AU-C section 600 requires the group engagement team to perform analytical procedures at the group level for any components that are not significant components. Depending on the circumstances of the engagement, the financial information of these components may be aggregated at various levels for purposes of the analytical procedures. The evidence from these analytical procedures corroborates the group engagement team's conclusions that no significant risks of material misstatement exist from the aggregated financial information of components that are not significant components. Therefore, the group engagement team may consider a number of factors when determining the aggregation level, as well as the nature, timing, and extent of the analytical procedures. Factors the engagement team may consider include, but are not limited to, group materiality, the risk of material misstatement of the group financial statements, and the nature and sufficiency of other audit evidence. For example, if the financial information of the components that are not significant components is at or near group materiality levels, the group engagement team may consider more in-depth or additional analytical procedures. Similarly, if the risk of material misstatement of the aggregated financial information of these components is low, the group engagement team may perform fewer analytical procedures or perform analytical procedures at a higher level.

.103 In situations in which no significant components have been identified, it is highly unlikely that the group engagement team will determine that analytical procedures at the group level are enough to obtain sufficient appropriate evidence to issue an audit report on the group financial statements. In these cases, as discussed in paragraph .63 of this alert, the group engagement team should assess what audit procedures could be applied, either to individual components or aggregations of components, in order to obtain sufficient audit evidence.

Specific Application Considerations—All Group Audits

> **Help Desk**: The following paragraphs will discuss in detail the additional or expanded audit procedures that are required under AU-C section 600 in all group audits. See paragraphs .139–.146 of this alert for additional requirements that are only applicable when the group engagement partner decides to assume responsibility for the work of a component auditor.

.104 A number of additional audit procedures are required under AU-C section 600, regardless of whether the group engagement partner decides to make reference to a component auditor in his or her report on the group financial statements. In addition, certain requirements in prior standards are expanded under AU-C section 600. These additional or expanded audit procedures may necessitate additional documentation and are discussed in the following paragraphs.

Overall Audit Strategy and Audit Plan

.105 Due to the new definitions and requirements of AU-C section 600, the group engagement team's approach to developing an overall group audit strategy and group audit plan may differ from that of previous years. The new definitions of *component, significant component,* and *component auditor* may affect the audit strategy and audit plan differently than under prior standards. For example, components and their component auditors may be identified well in advance of the planned timing of the engagement in order to make certain that the communications required under AU-C section 600 are adequate and occur on a timely basis. In addition, components that are significant due to their individual financial significance to the group are required to be audited (adapted as necessary to meet the needs of the group engagement team). These components may or may not have been audited at the level contemplated in AU-C section 600 in previous engagements performed under prior audit standards.

Understanding the Group, Its Components, and Their Environments

.106 Because the group engagement team is required to consider the risks of material misstatement (due to error or fraud) of the group financial statements, risk assessment procedures are necessary in the following areas, regardless of whether a component auditor will be involved:

- Identifying components, including significant components
- Gaining an understanding of the components
- Understanding and identifying group-wide controls
- Considering whether the group engagement team, the component auditor, or both need to perform tests of the group-wide controls
- Understanding the consolidation process (including the instructions issued by group management to components) and considering procedures the group engagement team, the component auditor, or both may perform

Understanding a Component Auditor

.107 Prior standards simply required the principal auditor (now the auditor of the group financial statements) to satisfy him- or herself about the independence and professional reputation of the other auditor (now component auditor) and to adopt appropriate measures to properly coordinate his or her activities with those of the other auditor whether referencing them or not in his or her audit report. In addition to required procedures related to the component auditor's professional competence, AU-C section 600 requires the group engagement team to perform additional procedures in connection with the component auditor that are related to (*a*) professional ethics; (*b*) the extent of involvement, if any, of the group engagement team in the work of the component auditor; (*c*) obtaining information from the component auditor related to the consolidation process; and (*d*) the regulatory environment in which the component auditor operates. These additional procedures may provide the group engagement team with information that could affect the risk assessment process, audit conclusions, or both. Such additional effort may vary depending on whether a component auditor is another firm or a member of the same firm as the auditor of the group financial statements. As such, it is important for the group auditor, as early as possible, to begin the process of understanding the component auditors and the level of cooperation expected. Failing to do so could lead to delays and undue pressure on the completion of the group audit.

.108 In certain circumstances (see paragraph .111 of this alert), AU-C section 600 does not allow the group engagement team to use the work of the component auditor and, by extension, does not allow the auditor of the group financial statements to assume responsibility for, or make reference to, the work of the component auditor in the audit report on the group financial statements. In such circumstances, the group engagement team is required to obtain sufficient appropriate audit evidence related to financial information of the component, without making reference to the audit of the component auditor or otherwise using the work of the component auditor, which may affect the group audit strategy, group audit plan, or both. AU-C section 600 applies both when the group engagement partner decides to make reference to the work of a component auditor and when the group engagement partner decides to assume responsibility for the work of a component auditor. Depending on the specific circumstances and the requirements of AU-C section 600, additional effort on the part of the group engagement team may be necessary, for example, when the

- component auditor does not meet the independence requirements relevant to the group audit. (The group engagement team may not use the work of the component auditor in any circumstance.)

- group engagement team has less than serious concerns about the component auditor's understanding of and compliance with the relevant ethical requirements or his or her professional competence. (The group engagement partner may not make reference to the component auditors' report but may use the component auditor, with adequate supervision, to perform certain procedures for which the group auditor assumes responsibility.)

- component's financial statements are not prepared using the same financial reporting framework as the group financial statements. (The group engagement partner may make reference to the component auditors' report if (1) the financial reporting framework used has measurement, recognition, presentation, and disclosure criteria that are similar to the group financial reporting framework and (2) the group auditor takes responsibility for evaluating the appropriateness of the conversion adjustments and reports appropriately. Otherwise, the group auditor may use the component auditor to perform an audit or procedures for which the group auditor takes responsibility.)

- component auditor has not issued a report stating that he or she performed an audit on the financial statements in accordance with GAAS or in accordance with the standards promulgated by the PCAOB. (The group engagement partner may make reference to the component auditors' report if the group auditor is satisfied that the audit performed by the component auditor meets the relevant requirements of GAAS; otherwise, the group auditor may use the component auditor to perform an audit or procedures for which the group auditor takes responsibility.)

- component auditor issued an auditor's report that is restricted as to use.[9] (The auditor of the group financial statements may not make reference to the component auditors' report.)

Determining Whether to Make Reference to a Component Auditor in the Auditor's Report on the Group Financial Statements

.109 The group engagement partner determines whether to make reference to the work of a component auditor in the audit report on the group financial statements. In developing the group audit plan, the group engagement team assesses, among other things, whether the auditor's report on the group financial statements will make reference to the audit of a component auditor. The group engagement partner (or the group engagement team) is required to communicate to those charged with governance the basis for the decision to make reference and may discuss the effect of this decision on the group audit strategy, group audit plan, or both with group management or those charged with governance of the group early in the planning phase of the group audit. Paragraph .A21 of AU-C section 600 provides additional considerations in this area that are specific to governmental entities. See paragraph .159 in this alert for further discussion of this requirement and practice issue as it relates to the audits of state and local governmental entities.

.110 Requirements in AU section 543 focused on the involvement of other auditors and when the principal auditor was able to assume responsibility for the work of other auditors. The requirements of AU-C section 600 focus on performing a group audit, including when the auditor's report on the group financial statements may reference the audit of a component auditor. AU-C section 600 requires that the group engagement partner, having gained an understanding of each component auditor, should decide whether to make reference to the component audit. This decision may also be based on the work performed by the group engagement team related to the audit strategy and plan as well as the understanding obtained with respect to the group, its components, and their environments. Under prior standards, this decision may have been made based on whether (*a*) the financial statements of the component were material in relation to the financial statements as a whole or (*b*) the other auditor (now the component auditor) was within or outside the network of the principal auditor (now the group auditor).

Help Desk: It's important that the group engagement team understand the group and its components, as well as the related assessed risks of material misstatement, in order to determine or evaluate whether the work of the component auditor will provide sufficient appropriate evidence to support the overall conclusion on the group financial statements.

.111 AU-C section 600 lists several conditions, summarized as follows, that should be met in order to make reference to the audit of a component auditor in the auditor's report on the group financial statements:

- The group engagement partner has determined that the component auditor performed an audit of the financial statements for the component in accordance with the relevant requirements of

---

[9] See footnote 4.

GAAS or, if applicable, auditing standards promulgated by the PCAOB. (Generally, this means complying with GAAS requirements related to planning and performing audits, rather than the form of the auditors' report. Audits conducted in accordance with ISA are more likely to comply with the relevant requirements.)

- The component auditor did not issue an auditor's report that was restricted as to use.[10]

- If the component financial statements were prepared using a different financial reporting framework than the group financial reporting framework, then the group auditor has determined that the component financial reporting framework has measurement, recognition, presentation, and disclosure criteria similar to those of the group financial reporting framework.

- The group engagement team has obtained sufficient appropriate audit evidence to enable it to determine that the reconciling adjustments necessary to convert to the group financial reporting framework are appropriate.

.112 The condition that component and group financial statements be prepared using the same financial reporting framework is not related to the type of entity. For example, group financial statements that combine for-profit entities and a not-for-profit entity that individually and collectively present financial information, as required by FASB, are considered to be prepared using the same financial reporting framework. Group financial statements of, for example, a state university using the financial reporting framework established by the Governmental Accounting Standards Board (GASB) and a not-for-profit entity using the financial reporting framework established by FASB are considered to be using the same financial reporting framework because GASB provides for the inclusion of component financial information prepared using a different financial reporting framework. However, group financial statements may consolidate an entity using the financial reporting framework established by FASB and an entity using the cash basis of accounting. In this case, the financial information prepared using the FASB financial reporting framework would not be considered to be presented using the same financial reporting framework as those entities using the cash basis of accounting. As such, the requirements noted in the preceding paragraph would be applicable.

.113 In certain group audit situations, (such as group audits of state and local governments with component units and not-for-profit organizations involving combined financial statements), components, at the component financial statement level, may be required to use a financial reporting framework that is different from the financial reporting framework used at the group financial statement level. See paragraphs .147–.161 of this alert for further discussion of this requirement and practice issue as it relates to the audits of state and local governmental entities.

.114 The auditor of the group financial statements is precluded from making reference to the work of a component auditor in the auditor's report on the group financial statements if the component auditor's report is restricted as to use. This condition may necessitate the group engagement team communicating with the component auditor early in the planning phase. If there is no

---

[10] See footnote 4.

requirement under GAAS for a component auditor to restrict the use of the report on the component, early communication with the component auditor may allow the component auditor to consider whether it is necessary to restrict the use of his or her report on the component's financial statements for other reasons.[11] If the group engagement partner is assuming responsibility for the component auditor's work and no reference is made, then a report on the component that is restricted as to use is not precluded from being considered as part of the group auditor's evidential matter.

.115 Requirements of AU-C section 600 are required to be applied in (a) audits of group financial statements and (b) compliance audits that may be required by federal, state, or local governmental regulations except for certain paragraphs of AU-C section 600, which are identified as not being applicable to a compliance audit in paragraph .A41 of AU-C section 935, *Compliance Audits* (AICPA, *Professional Standards*). A discussion of the requirements of the sections of AU-C section 600 that are applicable to a compliance audit is outside the scope of this alert.

.116 If any of the conditions discussed in paragraph .111 of this alert are not met, the auditor's report on the group financial statements cannot make reference to the work of the component auditor. In such circumstances, the auditor of the group financial statements assumes responsibility for the work of the component auditor. Therefore, the group engagement team may revise the group audit strategy, group audit plan, or both to perform additional audit procedures itself, or it may ask the component auditor to perform such procedures on its behalf. Additional time may be required to complete or to coordinate these additional procedures. Therefore, the group engagement partner may begin this decision process early in the audit planning phase of the group audit.

.117 When the group engagement partner decides to make reference to the audit of a component auditor in the auditor's report on the group financial statements, all of the provisions of AU-C section 600 apply except for those discussed in paragraphs .51–.65 of AU-C section 600. The requirements in those paragraphs are applicable to all components except those for which the auditor is making reference to the work of a component auditor. The group engagement team will need to be aware of the requirements that are applicable in each of these situations.

Materiality

.118 AU-C section 600 requires the group engagement team to determine materiality, including performance materiality, for (a) the group financial statements as a whole and (b) particular account balances, classes of transactions, or disclosures in certain circumstances. In addition, the group engagement team is required to determine materiality for components on which the group engagement team will perform, or for which the auditor of the group financial statements will assume responsibility for the work of a component auditor who performs, an audit or a review (adapted as necessary to meet the needs of the group engagement team).

.119 To implement these requirements, it will be necessary for the group engagement team to consider the following procedures:

- Identify all components.

---

[11] See footnote 4.

- Determine which components the group auditor will be directly responsible for auditing.
- Determine which components will involve the use of a component auditor. For each of those, determine which
  - the group auditor will accept the responsibility for the work of the component auditor.
  - the group auditor will make reference to in the auditors' report on the group financial statements.
- Determine which components are significant.

.120 Based on the information gathered in the preceding steps, the group auditor should then determine what materiality will be applied to

- the significant components for which the group auditor will be directly responsible.
- the significant components for which the group auditor will take responsibility for the work of the component auditor that
  - will be reviewed by the component auditor.
  - will be audited or have audit procedures performed by the component auditor.
- any components that are other than significant for which review or audit procedures will be performed.

For those components to which the group auditor is making reference, consider the impact on applied materiality.

.121 Based on the process outline in the preceding paragraphs, the next step is to develop a rational approach for applying materiality. The complexity of the process will depend on the number and type of components and the extent to which component auditors will be involved. The process will require extensive judgment. See example 2, "Multinational Manufacturing Company," in appendix D, "Applying Group Materiality to Components," for a case study that explores various approaches to the process.

.122 The group engagement team is required to establish component materiality at a lower materiality than that for the group financial statements. Different materiality may be established for different components, and the aggregate of component materiality may exceed group materiality.

Help Desk: AU-C section 600 does not require the group engagement team to communicate component materiality to the component auditor when reference to that component auditor will be made in the auditor's report on the group financial statements.

Responding to Assessed Risks

.123 In responding to the assessed risk of material misstatement, if the nature, timing, and extent of the work to be performed on the consolidation process or the financial information of the components is based on an expectation that group-wide controls are operating effectively, or when substantive procedures alone cannot provide sufficient appropriate evidence at the assertion level, the group engagement team is required in certain circumstances to test, or have a component auditor test on the group engagement team's behalf, group-wide controls over the (*a*) consolidation process or (*b*) financial information of the component. In other words, the control risk associated with the consolidation process or the financial information of a component is no different than the control risk associated with financial statement assertions in general. In order to place reliance on those controls, it is necessary to lower control risk sufficiently by testing the controls.

.**124** These requirements may affect the planned nature, timing, and extent of the work to be performed because AU-C section 600 may result in the identification of components, or significant components, not identified as such in previous engagements. The engagement team may find it helpful to determine if changes to the nature, timing, and extent of the planned work are necessary early in the risk assessment process in order to avoid potential delays in completing any related further audit procedures.

Consolidation Process

.**125** Specific procedures are required to be performed by the group engagement team or a component auditor on behalf of the group engagement team related to the consolidation process. The understanding of the consolidation process that the group engagement team obtains includes understanding the instructions issued by group management to components. Depending on the previous experience with the group, the group engagement team may find it helpful to review these instructions before they are disseminated to the components or early in the planning phase of the group audit. By reviewing the consolidation process instructions before they are disseminated, the group engagement team may be in a position to make recommendations to group management to improve the consolidation process. Additionally, such review may identify missing or ineffective consolidation controls that the group engagement team may consider when assessing the risk of material misstatement of the group financial statements. Items of interest may include the following:

- Reconciliations entries to the group financial reporting framework
- Foreign exchange adjustments
- Intracomponent accounts
- Related party adjustments
- Top side adjustments made to reflect acquisition accounting
- Reconciliation of component tax provisions to group tax provision

.**126** The group engagement team may also determine if all component financial information is expected to be prepared in accordance with the same accounting policies applied to the group financial statements early in the planning phase. Early communication with component auditors regarding differences in the application of accounting policies may result in audit efficiencies later in the engagement. For example, a component may use an asset capitalization threshold that is different from that used in the group financial statements. To adequately address the risk of material misstatement in such cases, the group engagement team may find it necessary to perform additional audit procedures or ask a component auditor to perform such procedures on its behalf. It will be more efficient if such procedures can be done in conjunction with the related areas in the audit of the component financial statements. See paragraph .161 of this alert for further discussion of this requirement and practice issue as it relates to the audits of governmental entities.

Subsequent Events

.127 Under GAAP promulgated by both FASB and GASB, management is responsible for determining the effect, if any, that subsequent events will have on the group financial statements. This extends to subsequent events affecting group financial statements, including those events affecting components that occur between the dates of the component financial information and the date the group financial statements are issued or available to be issued. The time period for which group management is responsible for subsequent events in the group financial statements may differ from the time period component management is responsible for subsequent events in the component financial statements or financial information. This would be the case in a group audit of a governmental entity that reports another entity as a component unit in its basic financial statements when the entities have different fiscal years. Further, the time period through which component management is responsible for subsequent events may be different than that of the group or component auditor. AU-C section 600 requires the group engagement team or component auditors to perform procedures to identify events at the components that occur between the dates of the financial information of the components and the date of the auditor's report on the group financial statements.

Help Desk: The group engagement team may put emphasis on audit procedures associated with subsequent events when components have a different reporting period than that covered by the group financial statements, or the component financial statements are issued at a different time than the group financial statements, because the risk of material misstatement of the group financial statements due to failure to properly account for subsequent events may be increased in such situations.

.128 AU-C section 600 will necessitate the group engagement team working closely with group or component management and with the component auditor in order to meet the professional responsibilities with respect to subsequent events. It will also likely call for the component auditor to work closer with component management. In some group audits, group management's ability to exercise control over component management may vary. This may create issues for the group engagement team and the component auditor in fulfilling the requirements of AU-C section 600 related to subsequent events. With respect to the subsequent event procedures, (*a*) the group engagement team may use the work of the component auditor, (*b*) both the group engagement team and the component auditor may perform procedures in this area, or (*c*) the group engagement team alone may perform procedures in this area. Regardless of the level of control group management may exercise over component management, the group engagement team and the component auditor have responsibilities for subsequent events under AU-C section 600.

Help Desk: Early communication with group management regarding its responsibilities to identify events at components that occur between the dates of the component's financial information and the date group management evaluates subsequent events for purposes of the group financial statements may increase audit efficiency for the group engagement team.

.129 Significant differences may exist between the reporting periods of the group and the components, or there may be differences in the dates of the auditors' reports on the group and one or more of the components. Therefore, the group engagement team may find it helpful to review the reporting periods of the group and the various components as soon as possible. Because group management is responsible for evaluating subsequent events, coordination between the group engagement team and the component auditor with respect to audit procedures related to subsequent events may help avoid duplication. The responsibilities of the group engagement team and the component auditor related to subsequent events may be agreed on by all parties and documented in order to avoid confusion at a later date. In addition, the auditor of the group financial statements may expand or modify the engagement or management representation letters for both the components and the group as a result of the requirements of AU-C section 600 relative to subsequent events.

.130 In situations in which the group engagement partner is making reference to the component auditor, it may be difficult to obtain the component auditor's agreement to comply with a request to notify the group engagement team about subsequent events. Nevertheless, the group engagement partner is required to consider the effect of subsequent events on the group financial statements, including all components. The group engagement partner may be able to obtain sufficient appropriate audit evidence through working with group management; examining group files related to the components, minutes, and budgets; and making appropriate inquiries.

Communication With a Component Auditor

.131 AU-C section 600 requires timely communication between the group engagement team and the component auditor of certain specific items and also requires that the communications about the group engagement team's requirements be documented. The group engagement team may also ask the component auditor to provide written documentation of any or all communications that AU-C section 600 requires of the group engagement team with respect to the component auditor (that is, whether the component auditor complied with ethical requirements—independence and professional competence—relevant to the group audit). Both the group engagement team and the component auditor may find it helpful to have all communications between them be in writing. For example, the group engagement team may ask the component auditor to confirm certain matters in writing. See paragraph .161 of this alert for further discussion of this requirement and practice issue as it relates to the audits of state and local governments.

.132 Due to the nature of some of the required communications, the group engagement team may wish to communicate certain items to the component auditor as soon as possible. The group engagement team may communicate its requirements to a component auditor when either (a) the component auditor is planning the audit or review of the financial information of the component that will be included in the group financial statements for the group's current financial reporting period (particularly when the entities have different fiscal years) or (b) the group engagement team is planning the audit of the group financial statements (whichever is earlier). For example, communication of related party information between the group engagement team and the component auditor provides both auditors with information that may be useful in executing the audit plan.

.133 AU-C section 600 does not explicitly establish requirements for the component auditor in audits of group financial statements. However, the engagement team is required to request a component auditor to communicate certain matters to it (often in a letter of instruction) and to evaluate the component auditor's communication (as well as the adequacy of his or her work). If effective two-way communication does not exist between the group engagement team and the component auditor, a risk exists that the group engagement team may not obtain sufficient appropriate audit evidence. However, the nature of some of the information that the group engagement team is required to request (for example, fraud, material misstatements, findings, conclusions, and so on) may prevent the component auditor from communicating it to the group engagement team before the component auditor has issued his or her overall findings, conclusions, or opinion. The group engagement team may establish a mutually agreed-upon time frame for the component auditor for the engagement period. In addition, the group engagement team may expand the group engagement letter to communicate to management and those charged with governance of the group the responsibilities of the component auditor under AU-C section 600.

.134 Situations involving auditors of equity method investees may present challenges in communicating with the component auditor because group management may not have the ability to influence management of the equity method investee or their auditors. The lack of effective communication with the component auditors does not in and of itself prevent the group auditor from making reference. However, the requirement to obtain an understanding of the component auditor with respect to ethical requirements, including independence, professional competence, and operation in an environment with regulatory oversight, and information about the consolidation process remain. Although it is more difficult without cooperation, it is possible if the component auditor operates in the same jurisdiction to obtain publically available information to assist in complying with the requirements.

Evaluating the Sufficiency and Appropriateness of Audit Evidence

.135 Under AU-C section 600, the group engagement team is required to evaluate the component auditor's communications (see paragraphs .131–.134 of this alert) and to discuss significant findings and issues arising from this evaluation with the component auditor, component management, or group management, as appropriate. Therefore, the group engagement team may find it helpful to have an in-depth discussion with the component auditor to discuss the requirements and expectations of the group engagement team with respect to the quality and timeliness of the component auditor's communications. This may be done as part of the planning phase of the group audit or before the planning phase begins, depending on the facts and circumstances of the timing of the group and component audits.

.136 In some cases, the group engagement team's evaluation of the component auditor's communication may indicate that additional audit procedures are necessary to provide sufficient appropriate evidence on which to base the group audit opinion. Therefore, the group engagement team may ask the component auditor, to the extent possible, to provide his or her communications well in advance of the planned date of the auditor's report on the group financial statements.

Communication With Group Management and Those Charged With Governance of the Group

.137 Several communications between the group engagement team and group management and those charged with governance for the group are required by AU-C section 600. Some of these communications, by their very nature, may occur before the engagement begins and some as part of wrapping up the audit of the group financial statements. These communications will generally address new requirements of the group engagement team. Consequently, the group engagement partner (or group engagement team) may discuss the requirements of AU-C section 600 with group management and those charged with governance of the group before or when the planning phase of the audit of the group financial statements begins.

.138 AU-C section 600 requires, among other communications, the group engagement team to communicate to group management and those charged with governance of the group the basis for the decision to make reference to the audit of a component auditor in the auditor's report on the group financial statements. Management and those charged with governance of the group may ask the group engagement partner what factors were considered in determining whether to make reference to a component auditor. Therefore, the group engagement partner or group engagement team may wish to be prepared to explain this decision to group management and to those charged with governance of the group.

Additional Requirements Applicable When Assuming Responsibility for the Work of a Component Auditor

> **Help Desk**: Paragraphs .139–.146 of this alert discuss the requirements of AU-C section 600 that are applicable only when the auditor of the group financial statements assumes responsibility for the work of the component auditor.

.139 Under AU-C section 600, the group engagement partner determines whether to make reference to a component auditor based on his or her understanding of each component auditor. In addition, AU-C section 600 provides that the component auditor should not be referenced in the auditor's report on the group financial statements unless certain conditions (see paragraph .111 of this alert) are met.

.140 When the auditor of the group financial statements assumes responsibility for the work of a component auditor (that is, there is no reference to the component auditor's work in the audit report on the group financial statements), AU-C section 600 provides for additional audit procedures specific to the component auditor's work. The new requirements of AU-C section 600 include both generic and specific procedures for significant components and those components that are not significant components as well as related documentation requirements.

> **Help Desk**: When the group engagement partner decides to assume responsibility for the work of a component auditor, AU-C section 600 requires a

(continued)

number of specific procedures that can be generally classified as relating to (1) involvement in the work performed by component auditors and (2) various required communications with a component auditor.

.141 AU-C section 600 requires that the group engagement team be involved in the risk assessment of a significant component, and the group engagement team's understanding of the component auditor affects the nature, timing, and extent of this involvement. AU-C section 600 describes minimum additional procedures that are required of the group engagement team primarily related to discussions with the component auditor and reviewing the component auditor's documentation of significant risks. These new requirements may result in the group engagement team spending more time than in previous engagements

- evaluating the risk of material misstatement,
- understanding the component auditor, and
- understanding the risk assessment done at the component level and the procedures the component auditor plans to perform to address them.

.142 When the auditor of the group financial statements assumes responsibility for the work of a component auditor who is performing an audit or review, there are communication requirements in addition to those required in all group audits. For example, the required written communication from the group engagement team to the component auditor requires communication of (a) component materiality; (b) the amount(s) lower than materiality for certain account balances, classes of transactions, or disclosures (if applicable); and (c) the threshold above which misstatements cannot be regarded as clearly trivial to the group financial statements. Determining and communicating these amounts early enough in the planning phase of the group audit may allow the component auditor to more adequately plan the nature, timing, and extent of his or her work on the financial information of the component.

.143 The group engagement team is required to request that the component auditor communicate some additional items in paragraph .61 of AU-C section 600 when the auditor of the group financial statements assumes responsibility for the work of the component auditor. Several of these items may affect the findings, conclusions, or opinion of the group engagement team related to the group audit. Consequently, the group engagement team and the component auditor may mutually agree upon a date by which this information will be communicated to the group engagement team. This provides the group engagement team with adequate time to evaluate the findings, conclusions, or opinion of the component auditor relative to the audit of the group financial statements.

.144 As discussed in preceding sections of this alert, AU-C section 600 requires the group engagement team to perform specific audit procedures related to significant components that may be considerably more extensive than those required or performed under prior standards when the auditor of the group financial statements is assuming responsibility for the work of a component auditor. For example, an audit of the financial information of a component, adapted as necessary to meet the needs of the group engagement team, is required for a component that is significant due to its individual financial significance to the group. Performing, or having these procedures performed, may require additional time and involve additional expense on the part of the group engagement team, component auditor, or both than in previous engagements.

.145 There is no requirement in AU-C section 600 that the group engagement partner obtain an audit or other report from a component auditor when assuming responsibility. Although many component auditors may issue a report with respect to their procedures, it is not required. The group engagement team may satisfy itself as to the level of work performed with a memorandum or summary of procedures from the component auditor or through its own review of the component auditors' working papers and related inquiries. A group engagement team may develop its own standard report that it requests the component auditor to complete.

.146 In some cases, component auditors have developed an internal policy whereby they furnish a report to the group auditor in accordance with the guidance in AU-C sections 800 or 805 depending on the circumstances and the work performed. Although this is not a presumptive requirement of the standard, the guidance in those AU-C sections may be helpful for group auditors in developing their own reporting protocol.

Considerations Specific to Audits of State and Local Governmental Entities

---

Help Desk: AU-C section 600 may have numerous implications for the auditor of governmental entities. Group and component situations may be created by the very nature of the reporting model for all levels of governmental entities. This section, however, discusses the implications AU-C section 600 may have for the auditor of a state or local governmental entity.

.147 GASB standards contain requirements for what is to be included in the state and local government financial reporting entity. Accordingly, the financial statements of state and local governments may include different legal entities or business activities and may have highly decentralized financial accounting or reporting systems. Furthermore, many of the different legal entities and business activities included in the governmental financial reporting entity may issue separate audited financial statements that are incorporated into the state or local government's basic financial statements. Therefore, AU-C section 600 will likely apply to many audits of state and local governments. The "Application and Other Explanatory Material" section of AU-C section 600 includes several references to requirements of AU-C section 600 that may warrant special consideration when auditing state and local governments. The AICPA Audit and Accounting Guide *State and Local Governments* provides guidance to assist auditors in auditing and reporting on those financial statements in accordance with GAAS. The guide will be updated for the clarity SASs, including the requirements of AU-C section 600, in 2013.

.148 AU-C section 600 applies to all audits of group financial statements, and because many state and local governments include component units in their financial statements, it is likely that AU-C section 600 may apply to a number of governmental entity audits.

.149 A number of areas in AU-C section 600 that may create challenges in implementing the requirements for all group audits have already been addressed in a general fashion in preceding sections of this alert. However, because the following areas are somewhat unique in audits of a state or local government's financial statements, additional discussion is provided in this section:

- Terms used in AU-C section 600 that are defined differently than certain similar terms used in the GASB literature

- Identification of *components* as defined in AU-C section 600 (see paragraph .A5 of AU-C section 600)

- Requirements to make reference to the audit of a component auditor in the auditor's report on the group financial statements (see paragraph .25 of AU-C section 600)

- The consolidation process, with respect to different accounting policies and different reporting periods (see paragraphs .37 and .39, respectively, as well as paragraph .A12 of AU-C section 600)

- Communication with a component auditor (see paragraphs .41– .42 of AU-C section 600)

Differences in Terminology

.150 The financial reporting framework for state and local governments uses terms and definitions that are similar to those used in AU-C section 600 but generally have a different meaning or context in the GASB literature. For example, GASB defines *component units* as legally separate organizations for which the elected officials of the primary government are financially accountable. Component units can also be other organizations for which the nature and significance of their relationship with a primary government are such that exclusion would cause the reporting entity's financial statements to be misleading. These separate legal entities are included in the primary government's basic financial statements (which may be group financial statements) as blended or discretely presented component units when certain conditions exist. However, *component units*, as defined by GASB, are not consistent with the definition of a *component* in AU-C section 600. The group engagement team may identify a component unit as a component under AU-C section 600, but it may also identify additional components because the definition of *component* in AU-C section 600 is broader than the GASB definition of *component unit*. For example, a major special revenue fund that is not a component unit but is required by GASB to be included in the governmental financial reporting entity's financial statements could, as defined by AU-C section 600, be identified by the group engagement team as a component that is a business activity.

.151 GASB defines *business-type activities* as those that are financed in whole or in part by fees charged to external parties for goods or services. Such activities, usually reported in enterprise funds, are an opinion unit for purposes of the government-wide financial statements. As discussed in AU-C section 600, business activities are those for which group or component management prepares financial information that is included in the group financial statements. In this context, the group engagement team may identify business-type activities in governmental financial statements as business activities; however, the existence of business-type activities does not necessarily indicate they are a component for purposes of applying AU-C section 600.

> **Help Desk**: The group engagement team will need to clearly understand the meaning of the terms used in AU-C section 600 and how they differ from the similar terms defined by GASB.

Identification of Components

> **Help Desk**: The auditor of the financial statements of a state or local government will need to understand the nature of the government's financial reporting entity, component units, and business activities, as well as the nature of any aggregated information, included in the government's financial statements in order to understand how, or if, the requirements of AU-C section 600 apply.

.152   A governmental financial reporting entity may represent a single governmental entity or a primary government and its component units, certain of which may be audited by different auditors or the same auditor. In addition, governmental component units may be an aggregation of several *components* as defined in AU-C section 600. Therefore, the group engagement team may identify *components* as defined in AU-C section 600 even if no component units are included in the reporting entity. Nothing precludes the group engagement team from aggregating either component units or components within a component unit or the primary government itself for purposes of reporting on the group financial statements. The group engagement team considers the composition of the governmental reporting entity, including its opinion units and auditors, to determine how AU-C section 600 applies. Auditors of state and local governmental entities may be government audit organizations, CPA firms and individuals, or both. See additional guidance in paragraph .A14 of AU-C section 600 related to considerations specific to governmental entities.

.153   Another unique feature of governmental entities that prepare their financial statements in conformity with the GASB financial reporting framework is that multiple reporting units are required to be included in the basic financial statements. AICPA Audit and Accounting Guide *State and Local Governments* discusses the various opinion units that the auditor considers and opines on separately in a state or local government financial statement audit. The auditor of the group financial statements, or a component auditor, may audit one or more opinion units. An opinion unit is not necessarily a component as described in AU-C section 600. For example, governmental and business-type activities are separate opinion units but, in a single general-purpose governmental entity using one financial accounting and reporting system for all its activities, may not necessarily be identified by the group engagement team as components.

.154   Some components included in a government's group financial statements may represent aggregated information from separate legal entities or *business activities* as defined in AU-C section 600. For example, the *business-type activities*, as defined by GASB and reported on the government-wide statements as an opinion unit, may be identified by the group engagement team as a component for purposes of the group financial statements. As such, this component would represent the aggregation of several enterprise activities or adjusted fund-level information.

.155 As mentioned, a component unit may be a component for purposes of AU-C section 600; however, a number of other, less easily identified components may exist within either the primary government or one of its component units (for purposes of the group financial statements). The group engagement team may apply the provisions of AU-C section 600 to the individual components or may conclude that it is more appropriate to identify components at aggregate levels for purposes of applying AU-C section 600. (Paragraphs .A3–.A4 of AU-C section 600 discuss levels of aggregation in components.) For example, the group engagement team may identify the utility fund of a general purpose government as a component rather than its separate business activities related to water, sewer, solid waste, and stormwater operations. Therefore, the group engagement team may spend additional time understanding the group, its components, and their environments in order to implement the requirements of AU-C section 600.

.156 The group engagement team may identify a number of components within the governmental financial reporting entity. However, business activities meet the definition of a *component* only if they represent business activities for which group or component management prepares financial information that is required by the GASB financial reporting framework to be included in the group financial statements of a state or local government. Business activities identified as components by the group engagement team may be those of the primary government or one or more of its component units.

> **Help Desk**: In group audits of state and local governments, the group engagement team may find it helpful to employ a "top down" approach to identifying components. An effective way to do this may be to ask group management what it considers to be components in the government's basic financial statements. For example, group or component management may aggregate information for the group financial statements using financial information that is prepared at a fund level based on the government's legal or administrative level of control. A key aspect of the definition of a *component* is the level at which group or component management prepares financial information for inclusion in the group financial statements.

.157 If only one auditor is responsible for reporting on all of the opinion units in the financial statements of a state or local governmental entity, the requirements of AU-C section 600 may or may not apply. The applicability of AU-C section 600 depends on whether more than one component is identified. Therefore, if more than one component is identified, the group engagement team is required to obtain an understanding of the group, its components, and their environments including group-wide controls (see paragraph .20a of AU-C section 600); establish a group audit strategy; and develop a group audit plan (see paragraph .18 of AU-C section 600). This understanding should be sufficient to confirm or revise the group engagement team's initial identification of significant components and to assess the risks of material misstatement (due to error or fraud) of the group financial statements. On the other hand, if only one auditor is responsible for all of the opinion units in the financial reporting entity and no components are included, the group engagement team could conclude that the financial statements are not group financial statements. In this situation, the audit of the government entity itself is not a group audit.

.158 In cases in which one auditor reports on the primary government and other auditors report on certain component units, the requirements of AU-C section 600 apply in the context of the group and the components identified by the group engagement team. AU-C section 600 allows the group engagement team to use significant judgment in determining components. Therefore, the group engagement team may want to keep this process as straight forward and high level as possible to increase audit efficiency. For example, if group or component management considers the component units as a business activity and that business activity is managed and accounted for using different systems from the primary government, the group engagement team may identify the component units as *components* (as defined in AU-C section 600) for purposes of applying AU-C section 600.

Help Desk: When evaluating business activities as potential components under AU-C section 600, the group engagement team may find it helpful to consider the level at which group or component management prepares financial information that is included in the group financial statements.

Reference to the Audit of a Component Auditor

.159 AU-C section 600 specifies conditions that should be met in order to make reference to a component auditor in the auditor's report on the group financial statements. One condition requires that if a component uses a different financial reporting framework than the group financial reporting framework, the measurement, recognition, presentation, and disclosure criteria of the components' financial reporting framework be similar to that used by the group. In some audits of governmental entities, this requirement may call for significant additional evaluation to determine if reference can be made to the work of a component auditor. To address the requirements, paragraph .A57 of AU-C section 600 provides that component financial statements are deemed to be in accordance with the applicable financial reporting framework when the applicable financial reporting framework provides for the inclusion of component financial statements that are prepared in accordance with a different financial reporting framework. For example, a governmental university prepares its group financial statements using the GASB financial reporting framework. The group financial statements include the financial statements of a foundation that is required by the GASB financial reporting framework to be included in the university's basic financial statements as a component unit. The foundation appropriately uses the FASB financial reporting framework and is audited by a component auditor. Assuming the other specific conditions are met, the auditor of the university's financial statements (group financial statements) is permitted to refer to the audit performed by the foundation's auditor (component auditor) because GASB provides for the inclusion of the foundation's FASB-based financial statements in the university's basic financial statements (see paragraph .A57 of AU-C section 600). As such, there would be no requirement to assess whether the component financial reporting framework was sufficiently similar to the group financial reporting framework. However, the group auditor is still required to evaluate the appropriateness of any adjustments to include the foundation's financial information in the university's financial statements.

Consolidation Process

.160 *Components*, as defined in AU-C section 600, in governmental group financial statements that are also component units for purposes of the reporting entity may have different management than that responsible for the group financial statements. Therefore, the financial information of a component may not be prepared in accordance with the same accounting policies applied to the group financial statements. For example, the period of availability used to recognize revenues by component management using the modified accrual basis of accounting may be different than that used by group management. Likewise, the asset capitalization threshold used by component management may be different from that used by group management. In such cases, the group engagement team may find it necessary to perform additional audit procedures or ask a component auditor to perform certain additional procedures on its behalf. This may be difficult in the audit of a governmental entity because the auditor of the primary government, acting as the auditor of the group financial statements, may have been appointed as a result of a competitive selection process with the scope of services and the related fees established for multiple years at the inception of the contract. In addition, this may be difficult when the auditor of the group financial statements does not have the jurisdictional authority to audit the component or when group management does not have effective or sufficient authority over the component. The group engagement team may determine that it is necessary in these situations to perform its own procedures on the financial information of such components. However, the group engagement team may be limited in the procedures it can perform unless the component is willing and able to engage the group engagement team.

Help Desk: The requirements of AU-C section 600 may be applicable regardless of the circumstances surrounding the engagement of the auditor of the group financial statements. The group engagement team may work with group management and the component auditor to effectively apply the requirements of AU-C section 600.

Communication With a Component Auditor

.161 As mentioned in the preceding paragraph, auditors for governmental entities may have been appointed through a competitive selection process. The existence of numerous auditors who are often competitors may hinder communication between the auditor of the group financial statements (that is, the auditor of the primary government) and the auditor of a component unit (identified by the engagement team as a component for purposes of applying AU-C section 600). The group engagement team may take into consideration the circumstances surrounding the relationship between the group engagement team and the component auditor when planning the group audit and developing the group strategy and group audit plan.

Resource Central

.162 Additional information and resources related to the Clarity Project are available on the AICPA Financial Reporting Center website at www.aicpa.org/FRC.

Publications

.163 Auditors may find the following publications useful. Choose the format that's best for you: online or print:

- AICPA Audit Risk Alert *Understanding the Clarified Auditing Standards—2012* (product no. ARACLA12P)

- Audit Guide *Analytical Procedures* (2012) (product no. AAGANP12P [paperback] or WAN-XX [online])

- Audit Guide *Assessing and Responding to Audit Risk in a Financial Statement Audit* (2012) (product no. AAGRAS12P [paperback], AAGRAS12e [eBook], or WRA-XX [online])

- Audit and Accounting Guide *State and Local Governments* (2013) (product no. AAGSLG13P [paperback] or WGG-XX [online with the associated Audit Risk Alert]).

- Audit Guide *Special Considerations in Auditing Financial Instruments* (2012) (product no. AAGAFI12P [paperback], AAGAFI12E [eBook], or AAGAFIO [online])

- Audit Guide *Auditing Revenue in Certain Industries* (2012) (product no. AAGREV12P [paperback], AAGREV12E [eBook], or WAR-XX [online])

- Audit Guide *Audit Sampling* (2012) (product no. AAGSAM12P [paperback], AAGSAM12E [eBook], or WAS-XX [online])

- Audit Risk Alert *Independence and Ethics Developments— 2012/13* (product no. ARAIET12P [paperback], ARAIET12E [eBook], or WIA-XX [online])

- *Audit and Accounting Manual* (2012) (product no. AAMAAM12P [paperback] or WAM-XX [online])

AICPA Online Professional Library: Accounting and Auditing Literature

.164 The AICPA has created your core accounting and auditing library online. The AICPA Online Professional Library is now customizable to suit your preferences or your firm's needs. Or, you can sign up for access to the entire library. Get access—anytime, anywhere—to FASB ASC, the AICPA's latest *Professional Standards*, *Technical Practice Aids*, Audit and Accounting Guides, Audit Risk Alerts, *Accounting Trends & Techniques*, and more. One option is the *AICPA Audit and Accounting Guides with FASB Accounting Standards Codification*, which contains all Audit and Accounting Guides, all Audit Risk Alerts, and FASB ASC in the Online Professional Library (product no. WFA-XX [online]). To subscribe to this essential online service for accounting professionals, visit www.cpa2biz.com.

Continuing Professional Education

.165 The AICPA offers a number of continuing professional education (CPE) courses that are valuable to CPAs working in public practice and industry, including the following:

- *Annual Update for Accountants and Auditors (2012–2013 Edition)* (product no. 730098 [text] or 180098 [DVD and manual]). Whether you are in industry or public practice, this course keeps you current and informed and shows you how to apply the most recent standards.

- *Internal Control Essentials for Financial Managers, Accountants and Auditors* (product no. 731859 [text]). This course will provide you with a solid understanding of systems and control documentation at the significant process level.

- *International Versus U.S. Accounting: What in the World is the Difference?* (product no. 745941 [text] or 181663 [DVD and manual]). Understanding the differences between IFRSs and GAAP is becoming more important for businesses of all sizes. This course outlines the major differences between IFRSs and GAAP.

.166 Visit www.cpa2biz.com for a complete list of CPE courses.

Online CPE

.167 AICPA CPExpress, offered exclusively through CPA2Biz, is the AICPA's flagship online learning product. AICPA members pay $209 for a new subscription. Nonmembers pay $435 for a new subscription. Divided into 1-credit and 2-credit courses that are available 24 hours a day, 7 days a week, AICPA CPExpress offers hundreds of hours of learning in a wide variety of topics. Some topics of special interest include the following:

- Accounting and auditing update
- Small business accounting and auditing update
- Fair value accounting
- Accounting for goodwill and other intangibles
- Uncertainty in income taxes
- Revenue recognition in today's business climate
- International versus U.S. accounting
- Fraud and the financial statement audit
- Public company update
- Securities and Exchange Commission reporting

.168 To register or learn more, visit www.cpa2biz.com.

Webcasts

.169 Stay plugged in to what is happening and earn CPE credit right from your desktop. AICPA webcasts are high quality, two-hour CPE programs that bring you the latest topics from the profession's leading experts. Broadcast live, they allow you to interact with the presenters and join in the discussion. If you cannot make the live event, each webcast is archived and available on CD-ROM. For additional details on available webcasts, please visit www.cpa2biz.com/AST/AICPA_CPA2BIZ_Browse/Store/Webcasts.jsp.

Member Service Center

.170 To order AICPA products, receive information about AICPA activities, and get help with your membership questions, call the AICPA Service Operations Center at 888.777.7077.

Hotlines

Accounting and Auditing Technical Hotline

.171   Do you have a complex technical question about GAAP, other comprehensive bases of accounting, or other technical matters? If so, use the AICPA's Accounting and Auditing Technical Hotline. AICPA staff will research your question and call you back with the answer. The hotline is available from 9 a.m. to 8 p.m. EST on weekdays. You can reach the Technical Hotline at 877.242.7212 or online at www.aicpa.org/Research/TechnicalHotline. Members can also e-mail questions to aahotline@aicpa.org. Additionally, members can submit questions by completing a technical inquiry form found on the same website.

Ethics Hotline

.172   In addition to the Technical Hotline, the AICPA also offers an Ethics Hotline. Members of the AICPA's Professional Ethics Team answer inquiries concerning independence and other behavioral issues related to the application of the AICPA Code of Professional Conduct. You can reach the Ethics Hotline at 888.777.7077 or by e-mail at ethics@aicpa.org.

.173

Appendix A—Questions and Answers

The following questions and answers are found in paragraphs .01–.41 of TIS section 8800, "Audits of Group Financial Statements and Work of Others" (AICPA, *Technical Practice Aids*), and are included here to provide nonauthoritative guidance regarding the implementation of AU-C section 600, *Special Considerations—Audits of Group Financial Statements (Including the Work of Component Auditors)* (AICPA, *Professional Standards*).

.01 Applicability of AU-C Section 600

Inquiry—Do the requirements of AU-C section 600, *Special Considerations—Audits of Group Financial Statements (Including the Work of Component Auditors)* (AICPA, *Professional Standards*), apply only when the auditor makes reference to the audit of another auditor in his or her report on the group financial statements?

Reply—No. AU-C section 600 applies to all audits of group financial statements. Certain requirements (detailed in paragraphs .50–.64 of AU-C section 600) are applicable to all components, except those for which the auditor of the group financial statements is making reference to the work of a component auditor. (See paragraph .08 of AU-C section 600.)

[Issue Date: November 2012.]

.02 Making Reference to Any or All Component Auditors

Inquiry—If the group engagement partner decides to make reference to one component auditor in the audit report on the group financial statements, is he or she required to make reference to all component auditors in that report?

Reply—No. The decision to make reference to the audit of a component auditor is made individually for each component auditor. The auditor of the group financial statements may make reference to any, all, or none of the component auditors. (See paragraphs .24 and .A52 of AU-C section 600.)

[Issue Date: November 2012.]

.03 Deciding to Act as Auditor of Group Financial Statements

Inquiry—What factors determine whether an auditor decides to act as the auditor of a group's financial statements?

Reply—The group engagement partner decides to act as the auditor of the group financial statements and report as such on the group financial statements upon evaluating whether the group engagement team will be able to obtain sufficient appropriate audit evidence through the group engagement team's work or use of the work of component auditors. Relevant factors in making this determination include, among other things, the (*a*) individual financial significance of the components for which the auditor of the group financial statements will be assuming responsibility, (*b*) extent to which significant risks of material misstatements of the group financial statements are included in the components for which the auditor of the group financial statements will be assuming responsibility, and (*c*) extent of the group engagement team's knowledge of the overall financial statements. (See paragraphs .15 and .A18 of AU-C section 600.)

In audits of state and local governments, additional factors to consider include (*a*) engagement by the primary government as the auditor of the financial reporting entity and (*b*) responsibility for auditing the primary government's general fund (or other primary operating fund). (See paragraph .A21 of AU-C section 600.)

[Issue Date: November 2012.]

.04 Factors to Consider Regarding Component Auditors

Inquiry—What factors might the group engagement partner consider when deciding to use the work of a component auditor and whether to make reference to the component auditor in the auditor's report on the group financial statements?

Reply—In all group audits, the group engagement team is required to obtain an understanding of the component auditor, and the group engagement partner uses this and his or her understanding of the component when deciding to use the work of a component auditor and whether to make reference to the component auditor in the auditor's report on the group financial statements. Factors affecting this decision include (*a*) differences in the financial reporting framework applied in preparing the component and group financial statements, (*b*) whether the audit of the component financial statements will be completed in time to meet the group reporting schedule, (*c*) differences in the auditing and other standards applied by the component auditor and those applied in the audit of the group financial statements, and (*d*) whether it is impracticable for the group engagement team to be involved in the work of the component auditor. (See paragraphs .22 and .A40 of AU-C section 600.)

[Issue Date: November 2012.]

[.05] Deleted

[Deleted, March 2013, due to the issuance of SAS No. 127, *Omnibus Statement on Auditing Standards—2013*. See section 8800.27, "Circumstances in Which Making Reference Is Inappropriate."]

.06 Governmental Financial Statements That Include a GAAP-Basis Component

Inquiry—When a governmental university includes a nongovernmental foundation as a component unit in its financial statements, as required by the Governmental Accounting Standards Board (GASB) financial reporting framework (that is, a not-for-profit foundation that appropriately uses accounting principles generally accepted in the United States of America [GAAP] as promulgated by the Financial Accounting Standards Board [FASB]), may the auditor's report on the university's group financial statements make reference to the auditor of the foundation's financial statements when the group engagement team identifies the foundation as a component?

Reply—Yes. In this situation, because the university (the primary government) is required by the GASB financial reporting framework to include the foundation as a component unit in the financial reporting entity (the group financial statements) and because GASB provides guidance on how to present component unit information that does not conform to GASB reporting standards, the financial statements of the foundation (a component) are deemed to be in accordance with the GASB financial reporting framework.

It is important to note that reference to a component auditor in these circumstances is appropriate only when the provisions established by GASB that require inclusion of the component unit in the financial statements of the primary government have been followed (see section 8800.27).

[Issue Date: November 2012; Revised: March 2013.]

[.07] Deleted

[Deleted, March 2013, due to the issuance of SAS No. 127. See section 8800.27.]

.08 Component Audit Performed in Accordance With Government Auditing Standards

Inquiry—When a component auditor conducts an audit of a component's financial statements using *Government Auditing Standards* (GAS), and the group engagement team conducts the audit of the group financial statements using generally accepted auditing standards (GAAS), may the auditor's report on the group financial statements make reference to the component auditor?

Reply—Yes. Financial audits performed under the 2011 revision of GAS incorporate AICPA Statements on Auditing Standards by reference, as well as establish additional requirements. Further, the audit reports issued to meet GAS requirements often refer separately to GAAS, as well. Therefore, the audit of the component would be deemed to have been performed in accordance with GAAS, and the audit report on the group financial statements may make reference to the component auditor. Such reference is appropriate only when the component auditor follows the requirements established by GAAS when conducting the financial audit of the component under GAS. (See paragraphs .25 and .A54 of AU-C section 600.)

[Issue Date: November 2012.]

.09 Component Audit Performed by Other Engagement Teams of the Same Firm

Inquiry—Do the requirements of AU-C section 600 apply when a CPA firm uses auditors in different offices of the firm to perform various audit procedures related to the audit of a single entity's financial statements?

Reply—If the group engagement team identifies components in the financial statements of a single entity, it is a group audit, and AU-C section 600 applies. As defined in AU-C section 600, a *component auditor* may be part of the group engagement partner's firm, a network firm of the group engagement partner's firm, or another firm. (See paragraph .11 of AU-C section 600.)

[Issue Date: November 2012.]

.10 Terms of the Group Audit Engagement

Inquiry—What matters are required to be included in the terms of the group audit engagement?

Reply—The auditor of the group financial statements is required to agree upon the terms of the group audit engagement. In addition to the matters identified in AU-C section 210, *Terms of Engagement* (AICPA, *Professional Standards*), other matters may be included in the terms of a group audit, including whether reference will be made to the audit of a component auditor in the auditor's report on the group financial statements. The terms of the engagement may also include arrangements to facilitate (*a*) unrestricted communication between the group engagement team and component auditors to the extent permitted by law or regulation and (*b*) communication to the group engagement team of important communications between (i) component auditors, those charged with governance of the component, and component management and (ii) regulatory authorities and components related to financial reporting matters. (See paragraphs .17 and .A28 of AU-C section 600.)

[Issue Date: November 2012.]

.11 Equity Method Investment Component

Inquiry—If a company has an investment accounted for using the equity method, is the equity method investment considered a component for applying AU-C section 600?

Reply—Yes. An investment accounted for under the equity method constitutes a component for purposes of AU-C section 600. As such, the requirements of AU-C section 600 apply; however, paragraphs .50–.64 of AU-C section 600 only apply when the group engagement partner assumes responsibility for the work of a component auditor. (See paragraphs .11 and .A2 of AU-C section 600.)

[Issue Date: November 2012.]

.12 Criteria for Identifying Components

Inquiry—What criteria might the group engagement team use to identify components?

Reply—A *component* is defined as "[a]n entity or business activity for which group or component management prepares financial information that is required by the applicable financial reporting framework to be included in the group financial statements." The structure of a group and the nature of the financial information and the manner in which it is reported affect how the group engagement team identifies components. Components can be separate entities or may be identified on the basis of the group financial reporting system that may be (*a*) a parent, one or more subsidiaries, and so on; (*b*) a head office and one or more divisions or branches; or (*c*) both. (See paragraphs .11 and .A1 of AU-C section 600.)

In audits of state and local governments, a component may be a separate legal entity reported as a component unit or part of the governmental entity, such as a business activity, department, or program. (See paragraph .A5 of AU-C section 600.)

[Issue Date: November 2012.]

.13 Criteria for Identifying Significant Components

Inquiry—What criteria might the group engagement team use to identify significant components?

Reply—A *significant component* is a component of individual financial significance to the group or likely to include significant risks of material misstatement of the group financial statements due to its specific nature or circumstances. As the individual financial significance of a component increases relative to the group financial statements, the risks of material misstatement of the group financial statements (posed by the financial information pertaining to that component) typically increase. The group engagement team may apply a percentage to one or more chosen benchmarks to identify components that are of individual financial significance. Appropriate benchmarks might include group assets, liabilities, cash flows, revenues, expenditures, net income, or a combination of these. Components engaging in complex transactions, such as foreign currency transactions, derivatives, alternative investments, complex financing arrangements, and so on, may expose the group to a significant risk of material misstatement even though they are not otherwise of individual financial significance to the group. The group engagement team may consider such components as significant components due to these risks. (See paragraphs .11, .A6, and .A77 of AU-C section 600.)

In audits of governmental entities, appropriate quantitative benchmarks for identifying significant components might include net costs or total budget. Qualitative considerations may involve matters of heightened public sensitivity (for example, national security issues, donor-funded projects, or reporting of tax revenue).

[Issue Date: November 2012.]

.14 No Significant Components Are Identified

Inquiry—Do the requirements of AU-C section 600 apply when the group engagement team does not identify any significant components?

Reply—Yes. AU-C section 600 is applicable to audits of group financial statements, and group financial statements include financial information for more than one component, regardless of whether any component is identified as a significant component. When a group consists only of components not considered significant components, the group engagement partner can reasonably expect to obtain sufficient appropriate audit evidence (on which to base the group audit opinion) if the group engagement team will be able to (*a*) perform work on the financial information of some of these components and (*b*) use the work performed by component auditors on the financial information of other components to the extent necessary to obtain sufficient appropriate audit evidence. In addition, when no component is identified as significant, it is more likely that appropriate responses to assessed risks of material misstatement for some or all accounts or classes of transactions may be implemented at the group level without the involvement of component auditors. (See paragraphs .A19, .A65, and .A83 of AU-C section 600.)

[Issue Date: November 2012.]

.15 Restricted Access to Component Auditor Documentation

Inquiry—When a component auditor restricts the group engagement team's access to relevant documentation, will the auditor of the group financial statements be able to report on the group financial statements?

Reply—Yes. As long as the group engagement team is able to obtain sufficient appropriate audit evidence, the group engagement partner is able to report on the group financial statements. However, this is less likely as the significance of the component increases. (See paragraphs .16 and .A23 of AU-C section 600.)

[Issue Date: November 2012.]

.16 Responsibilities With Respect to Fraud in a Group Audit

Inquiry—Does AU-C section 600 change the auditor's responsibilities with respect to fraud in the audit of a group's financial statements?

Reply—No. The group engagement team is required to gain an understanding of the group and its environment and to identify and assess the risks of material misstatement of the group financial statements due to error or fraud. In addition, the group engagement team is required to design and implement appropriate responses to the assessed risks. (See paragraphs .20 and .A35 of AU-C section 600.)

[Issue Date: November 2012.]

.17 Inclusion of Component Auditor in Engagement Team Discussions

Inquiry—Is the engagement team required to include the component auditor in its discussions of the entity's susceptibility to material misstatements of the financial statements due to error or fraud?

Reply—No. Key members of the group engagement team are required to discuss the susceptibility of an entity to material misstatements of the financial statements due to error or fraud, specifically emphasizing the risks due to fraud. The group engagement partner may choose to include the component auditor in certain discussions, including those to discuss the susceptibility of the entity to material misstatements of the financial statements. (See paragraphs .20 and .A36 of AU-C section 600.)

[Issue Date: November 2012.]

.18 Determining Component Materiality

Inquiry—If the group engagement partner decides to make reference to a component auditor in the auditor's report on the group financial statements, does the group engagement team establish materiality for the component auditor to use in the separate audit of the component's financial statements?

Reply—No. Reference in the group auditor's report to the fact that part of the audit was conducted by a component auditor is intended to communicate that the group auditor is not assuming responsibility for the work of the component auditor. In that case, the component auditor is responsible for establishing materiality as part of performing the audit of the component's financial statements.

However, if the group engagement partner assumes responsibility for the work of a component auditor, the group engagement team is required to evaluate the appropriateness of materiality at the component level. In addition, the group engagement team is required to communicate the relevant component materiality to that component auditor. The component auditor uses component materiality to evaluate whether uncorrected detected misstatements are material, individually or in the aggregate. (See paragraphs .31, .52–.53, .55, and .A73–.A74 of AU-C section 600.)

[Issue Date: November 2012.]

.19 Understanding of Component Auditor Whose Work Will Not Be Used

Inquiry—Is the group engagement team required to obtain an understanding of a component auditor for a component that is not a significant component if the group engagement team does not plan to use the work of the component auditor and plans only to perform analytical procedures at a group level?

Reply—No. It is not necessary to obtain an understanding of the auditors of those components for which the group auditor will not be using the work of the component auditor to provide audit evidence for the group audit. (See paragraphs .22, .29, and .A41 of AU-C section 600.)

[Issue Date: November 2012.]

.20 Involvement in the Work of a Component Auditor

Inquiry—When the group engagement partner decides to assume responsibility for the work of a component auditor, is the group engagement team required to be involved in the work of the component auditor?

Reply—Yes. The group engagement team is required to determine the type of work to be performed by the group engagement team (or a component auditor on behalf of the group engagement team) on the financial information of a component. The group engagement team is also required to determine the nature, timing, and extent of its involvement in the work of the component auditor. (See paragraph .51 of AU-C section 600.)

[Issue Date: November 2012.]

.21 Factors Affecting Involvement in the Work of a Component Auditor

Inquiry—What factors might affect the group engagement team's involvement in the work of a component auditor?

Reply—Factors that may affect the group engagement team's involvement in the work of a component auditor include (*a*) the significance of the component, (*b*) identified significant risks of material misstatement of the group financial statements, and (*c*) the group engagement team's understanding of the component auditor. (See paragraph .A84 of AU-C section 600.)

[Issue Date: November 2012.]

.22 Form of Communications With Component Auditors

Inquiry—When the group engagement partner decides to assume responsibility for the work of a component auditor, are all communications between the group engagement team and component auditor required to be in writing?

Reply—No. Communication between the group engagement team and a component auditor need not necessarily be in writing. For example, the group engagement team may visit the component auditor to discuss identified significant risks or review relevant parts of the component auditor's audit documentation. In all audits of group financial statements, however, communications between the group engagement team and component auditors about the group engagement team's requirements should be written. (See paragraphs .49, .59–.60, and .A87 of AU-C section 600.)

[Issue Date: November 2012.]

.23 Use of Component Materiality When the Component Is Not Reported On Separately

Inquiry—Is it necessary to use a component materiality lower than group materiality when the component will not be reported on separately, and the audit of the entire group is being performed by the group engagement team as one audit?

Reply—If the component is a significant component on which the group engagement team will be performing audit procedures, the group engagement team is required to determine component materiality. (See paragraph .31 of AU-C section 600.) To reduce the risk that uncorrected and undetected misstatements in each component's financial statements, when aggregated, do not exceed the materiality for the group's financial statements as a whole, component materiality should be less than the materiality for the group financial statements as a whole. In circumstances when appropriate responses to assessed risks of material misstatement for some or all accounts or classes of transactions may be implemented at the group level, for example when accounts receivable for the parent and subsidiaries use the same system and the consolidated accounts receivable are audited as one aggregated amount, there is no risk of aggregation error and, therefore, no need to allocate materiality to components.

[Issue Date: November 2012; Revised, February 2013.]

.24 Applicability of AU-C Section 600 When Only One Engagement Team Is Involved

Inquiry—Company X consolidates the operations of Entity A. The same group engagement team that audits Company X also audits Entity A. Because only one engagement team is involved, does AU-C section 600 apply? If so, what does AU-C section 600 require that is not already covered by other auditing standards?

Reply—AU-C section 600 applies to all audits of *group financial statements*, which are financial statements that contain more than one component. In the circumstances when the same engagement team audits all components of the group, the considerations addressed in AU-C section 600 that relate to component auditors are not relevant. However, considerations addressed in AU-C section 600, such as understanding the components; identifying components that are significant due to individual financial significance and the significant risk of material misstatement; determining component materiality; understanding the consolidation process; and addressing the risks, including aggregation risk, of material misstatement in the group financial statements; are relevant in all group audits.

[Issue Date: February 2013.]

.25 Applicability of AU-C Section 600 When Making Reference to the Audit of an Equity Method Investee

Inquiry—When the group engagement partner decides to make reference to the audit of the component auditor of an equity investee in the auditor's report on the group financial statements, is the group auditor still required to determine component materiality for those components for which reference to component auditors will be made?

Reply—Once the group engagement partner has decided to make reference to the audit of the component auditor, paragraph .26 of AU-C section 600 requires the group engagement team to obtain sufficient appropriate audit evidence with regard to the equity investee by

- performing the procedures required by AU-C section 600, except those required by paragraphs .50–.64.

- reading the equity investee's financial statements and component auditor's report thereon to identify significant findings and issues and, when considered necessary, communicating with the component auditor in this regard.

Therefore, when the group engagement partner has decided to make reference to the audit of a component auditor, the group engagement team is not required to determine component materiality for that component.

[Issue Date: February 2013.]

.26 Procedures Required When Making Reference to the Audit of an Equity Method Investee

Inquiry—The auditor of Company A has decided to make reference to the audit of the component auditor of an equity investee in the report on Company A's financial statements. In addition to obtaining and reading the equity investee's financial statements and component auditor's report thereon, what additional procedures may be necessary in order to determine that the equity investment has been properly recorded?

Reply—In determining that the equity investment has been properly recorded, the group engagement team may conclude that additional audit evidence is needed because of, for example, significant differences in fiscal year-ends, changes in ownership, or changes in conditions affecting the use of the equity method of accounting. Examples of procedures that the group engagement team may perform include, but are not limited to, reviewing information in the group's (investor's) files that relates to the equity investee, such as investee minutes, budgets, and cash flows information, and making inquiries of investor management about the equity investee's financial results.

[Issue Date: February 2013.]

.27 Circumstances in Which Making Reference Is Inappropriate

Inquiry—Are there any circumstances in which it would be inappropriate to make reference to the audit of a component auditor of an equity investee in the auditor's report on the group financial statements?

Reply—AU-C section 600 precludes the auditor of the group financial statements from making reference to the audit of the component auditor in the following circumstances:

- When the group engagement team has serious concerns about the component auditor's professional competency or independence. (In this circumstance, the group auditor is precluded from using the work of the component auditor at all.)
- The component auditor's report on the equity investee's financial statements is restricted regarding use.
- The audit of the component was not performed in accordance with the relevant requirements of GAAS or, if applicable, the standards promulgated by the Public Company Accounting Oversight Board (PCAOB).
- The financial statements of the component (that is, the equity investee) and group are prepared in accordance with different financial reporting frameworks, unless certain conditions are met.

Determining if the Audit of the Component Was Performed in Accordance With the Relevant Requirements of GAAS

When the component auditor has performed an audit of the component financial statements in accordance with auditing standards other than GAAS or the standards promulgated by the PCAOB, the group auditor is precluded from making reference, unless the group engagement partner has determined that the component auditor has performed an audit of the financial statements of the component in accordance with the relevant requirements of GAAS. Relevant requirements of GAAS in this context are those that pertain to planning and performing the audit of the component financial statements and do not include those related to the form of the auditor's report. Audits performed in accordance with International Standards on Auditing (ISAs) promulgated by the International Auditing and Assurance Standards Board (IAASB) are more likely to meet the relevant requirements of GAAS than audits performed in accordance with auditing standards promulgated by bodies other than the IAASB.

The group engagement team may provide the component auditor with AU-C appendix B, *Substantive Differences Between the International Standards on Auditing and Generally Accepted Auditing Standards* (AICPA, *Professional Standards*), that identifies substantive requirements of GAAS that are not requirements in ISAs.

The component auditor may perform additional procedures in order to meet the relevant requirements of GAAS. When the component auditor's report on the component's financial statements does not state that the audit of the component's financial statements was performed in accordance with GAAS or the standards promulgated by the PCAOB, and the group engagement partner has determined that the component auditor performed additional audit procedures in order to meet the relevant requirements of GAAS, the auditor's report on the group financial statements should clearly indicate

    a.   the set of auditing standards used by the component auditor and

    b.   that additional audit procedures were performed by the component auditor to meet the relevant requirements of GAAS.

Making Reference When Different Financial Reporting Frameworks Have Been Used

Conditions that, if met, permit the group auditor to make reference when the component financial statements are prepared in accordance with a different financial reporting framework than that used for the group financial statements are the following:

- The applicable financial reporting framework provides for the inclusion of component financial statements that are prepared in accordance with a different financial reporting framework, and as such, the component financial statements are deemed to be in accordance with the applicable financial reporting framework. For example, the financial reporting frameworks established by GASB and the Federal Accounting Standards Advisory Board have such provisions.

- The measurement, recognition, presentation, and disclosure criteria that are applicable to all material items in the component's financial statements under the financial reporting framework used by the component are similar to the criteria applicable to all material items in the group's financial statements under the financial reporting framework used by the group, and the group engagement team has obtained sufficient appropriate audit evidence for purposes of evaluating the appropriateness of the adjustments to convert the component's financial statements to the financial reporting framework used by the group without the need to assume responsibility for, and, thus, be involved in, the work of the component auditor.

When reference is made to a component auditor's report on financial statements prepared using a different financial reporting framework, the auditor's report on the group financial statements should disclose that the auditor of the group financial statements applied audit procedures on the conversion adjustments.

[Issue Date: February 2013.]

.28 Lack of Response From a Component Auditor

Inquiry—Paragraph .40 of AU-C section 600 requires the group engagement team to communicate to the component auditor and ask for his or her cooperation. Paragraph .41 of AU-C section 600 requires the group engagement team to ask the component auditor for certain information. If the component auditor does not respond to the group engagement team, is the auditor of the group financial statements precluded from making reference to the audit of a component auditor?

Reply—Lack of response from a component auditor to the communication and request for information from the group engagement team does not, in and of itself, preclude the group engagement partner from deciding to make reference to the audit of a component auditor. However, the group engagement team is required to obtain an understanding of the component auditor, in accordance with paragraph .22 of AU-C section 600, including

    a. whether a component auditor understands and will comply with the ethical requirements that are relevant to the group audit and, in particular, is independent.

    b. a component auditor's professional competence.

    c. whether the group engagement team will be able to obtain from a component auditor information affecting the consolidation process.

    d. whether a component auditor operates in a regulatory environment that actively oversees auditors.

Obtaining this understanding may be more difficult when the component auditor does not respond to the communication from the group engagement team. When a component auditor does not meet the independence requirements that are relevant to the group audit, or the group engagement team has serious concerns about the other matters previously listed, the group engagement team should obtain sufficient appropriate audit evidence relating to the financial information of the component without making reference to the audit of that component auditor in the auditor's report on the group financial statements or otherwise using the work of that component auditor.

[Issue Date: February 2013.]

.29 Equity Investee's Financial Statements Reviewed, and Investment Is a Significant Component

Inquiry—Company X has an equity investment in Entity A that the group engagement team has identified as a significant component. If the management of Entity A has their financial statements reviewed but refuses to allow an audit or any other work to be performed on Entity A's financial statements, does a scope limitation exist?

Reply—Yes. If Entity A is a significant component, and no auditing procedures can be performed on Entity A's financial statements, a scope limitation exists, and the effect of the group engagement team's inability to obtain sufficient appropriate audit evidence is considered in terms of AU-C section 705, *Modifications to the Opinion in the Independent Auditor's Report* (AICPA, *Professional Standards*).

[Issue Date: February 2013.]

.30 Making Reference to Review Report

Inquiry—Is it ever appropriate to make reference to another CPA's review report in an auditor's report on group financial statements?

Reply—No, it is never appropriate to make reference to the review report on the component's financial statements in the auditor's report on group financial statements. AU-C section 600 only provides for making reference to the audit of a component auditor.

[Issue Date: February 2013.]

.31 Review of Component That Is Not Significant Performed by Another Practitioner

Inquiry—Company X has an equity investment in Entity A that is not considered a significant component. A review of the financial statements of Entity A has been performed by another practitioner. Can the group engagement team use the work of the practitioner as part of the audit evidence for the audit of the group financial statements?

Reply—Paragraphs .54–.55 of AU-C section 600 discuss certain procedures to be performed on a component when the component is not a significant component. In certain circumstances, a review of a component's financial statements may be sufficient audit evidence. Therefore, a group auditor may use the work of another practitioner if the review meets the needs of the group auditor. Although the group auditor may use the review as part of the auditor's evidence for the audit of the group financial statements, the group auditor is not permitted to make reference to the practitioner's review report.

[Issue Date: February 2013.]

.32 Issuance of Component Auditor's Report

Inquiry—Company X has an investment in Entity A accounted for under the equity method of accounting. Company X is audited by one firm, and a CPA from a different firm performs audit procedures at Entity A sufficient to provide the auditor of Company X with appropriate audit evidence relative to the equity investee's financial information. Is it necessary for the auditor of Company X to obtain an auditor's report on Entity A's financial statements from the component auditor?

Reply—Although an audit report is typically obtained when an independent CPA performs work for a group auditor of a different firm, there is no requirement that such report be obtained if the group auditor assumes responsibility for the component auditor's work. When the auditor of Company X will assume responsibility for, and, thus, be involved in, the work of a component auditor, a component auditor's communication with the group engagement team may take the form of a memorandum or report of work performed. Alternatively, the auditor of Company X may decide to review the component auditor's working papers documenting the audit procedures performed. However, in order for the auditor of Company X to make reference to the audit of the component auditor, it is necessary for the component auditor to issue an auditor's report on Entity A.

[Issue Date: February 2013.]

.33 Structure of Component Auditor Engagement

Inquiry—Company X has an investment in Entity A accounted for under the equity method of accounting. Entity A is not willing to pay for an audit of its financial statements. Would an agreed-upon procedures engagement performed by an independent CPA for Entity A be sufficient to provide the auditor of Company X with appropriate audit evidence relative to the investment in the equity investee?

Reply—The auditor of Company X is responsible for determining the nature and extent of the procedures necessary to provide the auditor of Company X with sufficient appropriate audit evidence relative to the investment in the equity investee. The nature and extent of the necessary procedures are based on the significance of the component to the group. A component auditor may perform specified audit procedures relating to the likely significant risks of material misstatement of the group financial statements on behalf of the auditor of Company X. However, the structure of the engagement for the component auditor to perform the necessary procedures is not addressed by the standard.

[Issue Date: February 2013.]

.34 Subsequent Events Procedures Relating to a Component

Inquiry—Company X has an investment in Entity A that is accounted for by the equity method of accounting. Company X and Entity A are audited by different auditors. The audit of Entity A was completed before the audit of Company X began, and the auditor of Company X's financial statements has decided to make reference to the report of the auditor of Entity A. In such circumstances, who is responsible for performing auditing procedures relating to subsequent events at Entity A that may require adjustment to, or disclosure in, the group financial statements?

Reply—The auditor of the group financial statements is responsible for obtaining sufficient appropriate audit evidence that the group financial statements are free from material misstatement, regardless of whether reference is made to the audit of a component auditor. Paragraph .39 of AU-C section 600 states that for components that are audited, the group engagement team or component auditors should perform procedures designed to identify events at those components that occur between the dates of the financial information of the components and the date of the auditor's report on the group financial statements and that may require adjustment to, or disclosure in, the group financial statements.

When the audit of the component is completed before the date of the auditor's report on the group financial statements, the group engagement team may communicate with the component auditor and ask the component auditor to perform procedures to identify subsequent events that would require adjustment to, or disclosure in, the group financial statements. Alternatively, the group engagement team may work with group management to obtain the necessary information and perform procedures themselves. Examples of procedures the group engagement team may perform include, but are not limited to, reviewing information in group management's files that relates to the component, such as component minutes, budgets, and cash flows information, and making inquiries of group management about the component's financial results.

If the group engagement team is unable to obtain sufficient appropriate audit evidence about subsequent events to make a determination about whether the group financial statements are materially misstated, then a scope limitation exists, and the effect of the group engagement team's inability to obtain sufficient appropriate audit evidence is considered in terms of AU-C section 705.

[Issue Date: February 2013.]

.35 Component and Group Have Different Year-Ends

Inquiry—Company X has a component comprising an investment in Entity A accounted for by the equity method of accounting. Entity A is audited by a component auditor. Entity A has a different year-end than Company X. The auditor of the group financial statements has decided to make reference to the audit of the component auditor. What procedures, if any, would be appropriate for the group engagement team perform as a result of the difference in year-ends?

Reply—FASB *Accounting Standards Codification* (ASC) 323-10-35-6 states that "[i]f financial statements of an investee are not sufficiently timely for an investor to apply the equity method currently, the investor ordinarily shall record its share of the earnings or losses of an investee from the most recent available financial statements. A lag in reporting shall be consistent from period to period." When a time lag in reporting between the date of the financial statements of the group and that of the component exists, appropriate procedures performed by the group engagement team include consideration of whether the time lag is consistent with the prior period in comparative statements and, as discussed in section 8800.15, "Restricted Access to Component Auditor Documentation," whether a significant transaction occurred during the time lag that would require adjustment to, or disclosure in, the group financial statements. The group engagement team may also perform auditing procedures on the information from the period audited by the component auditor to Company X's year-end (stub period). If the group engagement team is unable to obtain sufficient appropriate audit evidence about the stub period information, a scope limitation exists, and the effect of the group engagement team's inability to obtain sufficient appropriate audit evidence is considered in terms of AU-C section 705. If a change in stub period occurs that has a material effect on the group's financial statements, the auditor should consider the consistency of the financial statements for the periods presented, in accordance with AU-C section 708, *Consistency of Financial Statements* (AICPA, *Professional Standards*), because of the change in reporting period.

[Issue Date: February 2013.]

.36 Investments Held in a Financial Institution Presented at Cost or Fair Value

Inquiry—Paragraph .11 of AU-C section 600 defines a component as "[a]n entity or business activity for which group or component management prepares financial information that is required by the applicable financial reporting framework to be included in the group financial statements." Is an investment in a certificate of deposit or other types of cash investments held by a financial institution (for example, an overnight repurchase agreement) deemed a component for purposes of AU-C section 600?

Reply—No. A certificate of deposit or other cash investments held by a financial institution or bank do not constitute components.

[Issue Date: February 2013.]

.37 Employee Benefit Plan Using Investee Results to Calculate Fair Value

Inquiry—Do the investments in an employee benefit plan that rely on the investee results to calculate fair value constitute components under AU-C section 600?

Reply—No. Generally, the investments held by an employee benefit plan are required to be accounted for at fair value, with limited exceptions, and do not constitute a *component*, as defined under AU-C section 600; therefore, AU-C section 600 would not apply.

[Issue Date: February 2013.]

.38 Using Net Asset Value to Calculate Fair Value

Inquiry—Paragraphs 59–62 of FASB ASC 820-10-35 permit a reporting entity to estimate the fair value of an investment using net asset value (NAV) per share of the investment (or its equivalent) if NAV is calculated in a manner consistent with the measurement principles of FASB ASC 946, *Financial Services—Investment Companies*, as of the reporting entity's measurement date. If an entity uses the NAV of an investment as a practical expedient to estimate the fair value of that investment, is that investment considered a component under AU-C section 600?

Reply—No. Paragraph .A2 of AU-C section 600 states that an investment accounted for under the equity method constitutes a component for purposes of AU-C section 600. AU-C section 600 does not specifically identify what other, if any, types of investments may be considered components under the definition in that section.

When an entity elects to use NAV as a practical expedient, paragraph .04 of AU-C section 501, *Audit Evidence—Specific Considerations for Selected Items* (AICPA, *Professional Standards*), generally applies because it addresses situations when investments in securities are valued based on an investee's financial results, excluding investments accounted for using the equity method of accounting.

Paragraph .04 of AU-C section 501 states that when investments in securities are valued based on an investee's financial results, excluding investments accounted for using the equity method of accounting, the auditor should obtain sufficient appropriate audit evidence in support of the investee's financial results, as follows:

    a.   Obtain and read available financial statements of the investee and the accompanying audit report, if any, including determining whether the report of the other auditor is satisfactory for this purpose.

    b.   If the investee's financial statements are not audited or if the audit report on such financial statements is not satisfactory to the auditor, apply or request that the investor entity arrange with the investee to have another auditor apply appropriate auditing procedures to such financial statements, considering the materiality of the investment in relation to the financial statements of the investor entity.

    c.   If the carrying amount of the investment reflects factors that are not recognized in the investee's financial statements or fair values of assets that are materially different from the investee's carrying amounts, obtain sufficient appropriate audit evidence in support of such amounts.

d. If the difference between the financial statement period of the entity and investee has or could have a material effect on the entity's financial statements, determine whether the entity's management has properly considered the lack of comparability, and determine the effect, if any, on the auditor's report.

[Issue Date: February 2013.]

.39 Disaggregation of Account Balances or Classes of Transactions

Inquiry—Company X consolidates the operations of Entity A. The same group engagement team audits Company X and the operations of Entity A; no other auditors or engagement teams are involved. Are there any requirements in AU-C section 600 to disaggregate account balances or classes of transactions for purposes of auditing the consolidated financial statements of Company X? For example, is the auditor required to disaggregate accounts receivable for purposes of confirmation procedures, or can the consolidated group of accounts be treated as one population?

Reply—AU-C section 600 does not require the auditor to disaggregate account balances or classes of transactions. The group auditor should design an audit plan that is responsive to the risks of material misstatements to the consolidated financial statements. The less similar the risks of material misstatement at the group and component level, the less appropriate it may be to perform audit procedures for some or all accounts or classes of transactions at the group level. Additionally, the more complex the group (for example, decentralized systems, fewer groupwide controls, differing jurisdictions, or diverse product lines), the less likely that testing in the aggregate will sufficiently and appropriately address the risks of material misstatement.

[Issue Date: February 2013.]

.40 Variable Interest Entities (VIEs) as a Component

Inquiry—Company X consolidates the financial information of Entity A, a variable interest entity of which Company X is the primary beneficiary. Is Entity A considered a component for purposes of AU-C section 600?

Reply—Yes. Paragraph .11 of AU-C 600 defines a component as "[a]n entity or business activity for which group or component management prepares financial information that is required by the applicable financial reporting framework to be included in the group financial statements." Because Entity A's financial information is required to be consolidated into Company X's financial statements, Entity A constitutes a component for purposes of AU-C section 600. As such, the requirements of AU-C section 600 apply.

[Issue Date: March 2013.]

.41 Component Using a Different Basis of Accounting Than the Group

Inquiry—A component whose financial information is required to be consolidated into group financial statements maintains its financial information on the tax basis of accounting. The group financial statements are prepared using GAAP. What is the group auditor's responsibility regarding the consolidation of the component's financial information into the group financial statements?

Reply—When a component's financial information is prepared on the tax basis of accounting, and the group financial statements are prepared using

GAAP, the auditor is required by paragraph .36 of AU-C section 600 to evaluate whether the financial information of the component has been appropriately adjusted. Appropriate adjustments are adjustments that convert the tax basis of information to GAAP basis. An example of this is converting depreciation under the method used for tax purposes by the component to depreciation calculated using the method used for the group financial statements.

[Issue Date: March 2013.]

.174

Appendix B—Decision-Making Flowchart

AU-C section 600, *Special Considerations—Audits of Group Financial State-ments (Including the Work of Component Auditors)* (AICPA, *Professional Stan-dards*), establishes specific requirements related to components that the group engagement team identifies as significant and those that are not significant (discussed in paragraphs .61–.63 of this alert). The following flowchart, found in paragraph .A79 of AU-C section 600, depicts how the significance of the component affects the group engagement team's determination of the type of work to be performed on the financial information of the component.

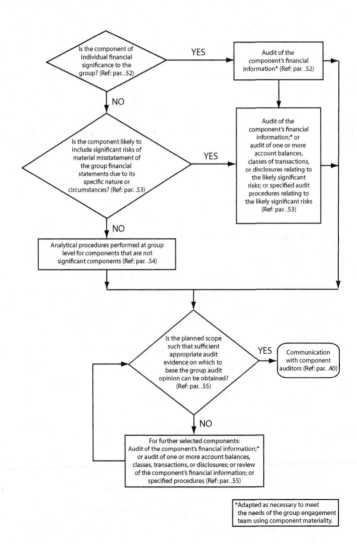

.175

Appendix C—Examples

Example 1—Not-for-Profit University With Consolidated Financial Statements, Two Auditors, and Different Reporting Periods

Facts

A not-for-profit university (University) prepares consolidated financial statements (in accordance with the requirements in Financial Accounting Standards Board Accounting Standards Codification 958-810) that include consolidated financial information for the University, its legally separate not-for-profit foundation (Foundation), and its legally separate but related alumni association (Association). The Foundation and Association provide services that directly benefit the university or its students, alumni, or faculty. To prepare the consolidated financial statements, the University uses the information provided in the audited financial statements of the separate entities.

Both the University and the Foundation are required to have an annual audit of their financial statements by state statute and by their respective corporate bylaws. After a competitive selection process, CPA Firm A was appointed to a five-year contract by the joint university-foundation audit selection committee two years ago to audit both the University and the Foundation. For the current year, CPA Firm A will audit the June 30, 2013, financial information of the University and the Foundation, as well as the consolidated financial statements as of June 30, 2013.

CPA Firm B was selected by the Association's board of directors as the independent auditor years ago upon creation of the Association. An annual audit of the Association's financial statements is required by the Association's corporate bylaws. The Association does not have an audit committee because the board of directors feels it provides adequate oversight of financial reporting and the auditor selection process. Audited financial information for the year ended December 31, 2012, will be adjusted through June 30, 2013, and included in the combined financial statements as of June 30, 2013. Historically, CPA Firm A has used the Association's audited financial statements as audit evidence for the consolidated financial statements and has made reference to the work of CPA Firm B in the auditor's report on the consolidated financial statements.

In addition to education and the related administrative support activities, significant business activities of the University include parking, housing, a book store, and food service operations. All of these services except parking are performed under contracts with various private-sector entities. Information related to the contract activities is as follows:

- *Housing.* The University owns all dorms, equipment, and furnishings, and the contractor provides cleaning and routine maintenance services for all facilities under contract. In addition, the contractor processes student housing requests and assignments (applications, selection and assignment of students, executing student housing contracts, pre- and post-inspections of student rooms) and sends an electronic file to the University with all student room and billing information. The University bills each student for room and board on the individual student's tuition statement at the beginning of each term. Each month, the University pays the contractor a set fee for each application processed and a set fee per dorm resident for operating and maintaining the dorms. Amounts remitted to the contractor are based on student population information maintained by the University.

- *Book store.* The contractor provides a full turn-key operation, and in return the contractor pays the University a monthly commission based on the previous month's sales. The contractor provides a monthly sales and returns summary report to the University's business services department (Business Services) that details the calculation of the amount remitted. Business Services records commission revenue upon receipt of the contractor's payment through the University's financial management system. Under the terms of the contract, the University has the authority to review the contractor's operations and sales records at any point with proper notice to the contractor. The contract requires the contractor to provide the University with an annual summary of monthly sales and returns by type within 30 days of the University's fiscal year end. In addition, the contract requires that the information be subject to certain agreed-upon procedures that are performed by and reported on by the contractor's auditor (CPA Firm C). Business Services recalculates the commission revenue using this information and compares it to the amounts reported and remitted for the year.

- *Food service.* The University owns and maintains all food service-related facilities, equipment, and furnishings with routine maintenance provided and arranged by the buildings and grounds department through the University work order system at the request of the contractor. All purchases and sales are processed through various automated and integrated systems of the University by the contractor. The contractor uses the University's integrated purchase order system for ordering food and supplies and a point-of-sale register system that is integrated with the University's cash receipts system. A perpetual inventory system is owned and operated by the contractor, and a quarterly inventory is conducted by the contractor under the supervision and direction of Business Services. Under terms of the contract, the University has the authority to review any of the contractor's operations at any point in time. Employees working in the food service operation are hired, scheduled, and paid by the contractor. Each month the University pays the contractor an agreed-upon administrative charge, which is calculated by Business Services using sales and purchases information generated by the University's financial management system.

Activities conducted by the Foundation include fund raising, community awareness, and advocacy all for the exclusive benefit of the Foundation and the University. In addition, the Foundation provides portfolio management services for all of the Foundation and University board and donor designated endowment funds. The Foundation charges a management fee for these services that is deducted from the earnings recorded by the endowment funds. The University provides a contractually agreed-upon contribution each year to help defray the Foundation's operating costs. All activities are accounted for and recorded by the Foundation.

The Association is housed in a separate building on campus that is owned and maintained by the University. The University provides a contractually agreed-upon contribution each year to help defray the Association's operating costs. All activities are accounted for and recorded by the Association. Business activities of the Association include sponsoring alumni social, educational, and informational events; conducting fundraising activities for the benefit of the Association; and communicating on a regular basis with alumni about other alumni-related activities.

Commentary

This is a *group audit* as defined in AU-C section 600, *Special Considerations— Audits of Group Financial Statements (Including the Work of Component Auditors)* (AICPA, *Professional Standards*), because the consolidated financial statements represent group financial statements; that is, they include financial information for more than one component (financial information for the University, the Foundation, and the Association).

The components in this example could be identified by the group engagement team as the three separate legal entities for which financial information is included in the consolidated financial statements: the University, Foundation, and Association. It is likely not efficient to identify business activities as components in this example because the group financial statements are prepared using the entity-level audited financial statements (financial information) rather than financial information at the business activity level (see paragraph .A1 of AU-C section 600). The housing, book store, and food service business activities would likely be considered in the risk assessment process related to the audit of the financial statements of the University by CPA Firm A. Business activities of the Association would also likely be considered in the risk assessment process related to the audits of those individual financial statements by CPA Firm B.

Additionally, more than one auditor is performing work on the financial information that is included in the group financial statements (consolidated financial statements). In this example, CPA Firm A is responsible for the consolidated financial statements (that is, the group audit engagement) and would therefore be the auditor of the group financial statements (see paragraph .11 of AU-C section 600). As the auditor of the Association's financial statements, CPA Firm B would be a component auditor. In addition, in the group audit of the consolidated financial statements of the University and the Foundation, the staff members of CPA Firm A assigned to the audit of the Foundation's financial statements would each meet the definition of a component auditor for purposes of that audit (see paragraph .A11 of AU-C section 600). The group engagement partner would decide whether to make reference to the audit report of CPA Firm B in the audit report on the group financial statements (consolidated financial statements).

CPA Firm C would not be considered a component auditor because the financial information included in the group financial statements (consolidated financial statements) is aggregated at an entity level rather than a business activity level. Additionally, the financial information on which CPA Firm C performs the agreed-upon procedures is not used to record the financial information related to the book store (business activity). Business Services simply uses the information to affirm the amount of commissions received for the fiscal year.

Example 2—Private Sector Entity With Multiple Locations and Business Activities, Same Auditor Using Different Firm Offices

Facts

A multi-office CPA firm provides audit services for a medium-sized privately held company that has significant operations in three states. The company has a central distribution center located in Arkansas and a regional sales office located in Georgia. Administrative offices, as well as another regional sales office, are located at the company's corporate headquarters in California.

The company reports operating, performance, and selected financial information at a division level for the distribution center and the two sales offices. All other operating and financial information is aggregated and reported at a corporate-wide level. Divisional and corporate level information for the company is as follows:

- *Regional sales offices.* Each regional sales office has a domestic and an international division. Domestic sales account for approximately 80 percent of the company's total annual sales. Various personnel at each regional sales office account for all customer and sales order transactions using the company's integrated operations management system. No shipping, billing, or collection information is processed at the regional sales offices. Executive leadership at the administrative office develops the pricing structure and schedule used by the regional sales offices in soliciting orders. In prior years, the auditor identified significant risks at both offices due to missing or ineffective controls, including little oversight and training.

- *Central distribution center.* The distribution center has three divisions: purchasing, receiving, and shipping. Shipments are made using sales order information entered in the integrated operations management system by personnel at the regional sales offices. A perpetual inventory system is maintained by the receiving division, but it is not integrated with the company's financial accounting system. Various personnel in the three divisions at the central distribution center account for all transactions occurring at the distribution center using the company's integrated operations management system. The company does not enter into long term purchase commitments.

  Certain aspects of the company's integrated operations management system interface with the financial accounting system. Purchases are integrated in the company's financial accounting system when the goods are noted as being received in the integrated operations management system by personnel in the receiving division. Customer information entered at the regional sales offices and shipping information entered by the shipping division at the central distribution center are integrated with the customer billing subsystem that is integrated with the financial accounting system. All customer billing is done by the accounting department (located at the company's headquarters) using the customer billing subsystem. Each month the receiving division provides ending inventory information to the accounting department, at which point it is recorded as one amount in the company's financial accounting system. No significant risks related to the distribution center have been identified by the auditor in prior years.

- *Administration.* All executive, finance, accounting, and financial reporting and human resources functions are conducted at the corporate headquarters in California. In addition to developing the pricing structure and schedule, the executive office maintains price master file information that integrates with shipping information during the customer billing process. The company uses a lock box system for the receipt and processing of all customer receipts (electronic funds transfers or checks), which are downloaded daily by the accounting department into the company's financial accounting system.

The engagement partner and engagement team work in the CPA firm's California office; accordingly, the CPA firm's California office will coordinate the audit of, and report on, the financial statements for the year ended December 31, 2012. As in prior year audits, the audit strategy will be developed by the engagement team and will include using personnel in the CPA firm's Georgia and Arkansas offices to perform certain procedures at the company's Georgia regional sales office and central distribution center, respectively. The engagement team will develop the audit plan and coordinate and oversee the work performed by the Georgia and Arkansas offices of the CPA firm.

Personnel in the CPA firm's Arkansas office will be utilized by the engagement team to observe the annual inventory and perform test counts. In addition, the Arkansas office personnel will be utilized to perform risk assessment procedures related to all operations and to perform control tests for certain processes related to the receiving division of the central distribution center. The engagement team will utilize personnel in the CPA firm's Georgia office to perform risk assessment procedures and further audit procedures (tests of controls and substantive tests of details), all of which will be developed by the engagement team. Members of the engagement team will perform risk assessment procedures and further audit procedures (tests of controls and substantive tests of details) for the California regional sales office.

Commentary

This is a *group audit* as defined in AU-C section 600 because there is more than one component (based on business activities defined as either geographic locations or operating activities or divisions). This example is depicting the identification of components by function or process.

The accounting and financial reporting function at the administrative office and the receiving division at the central distribution center are components because they provide financial information that is required to be included in the group financial statements by the financial reporting framework. The receiving division provides purchasing and ending inventory information that is used to record inventory, accounts payable, and cost of goods sold, all of which are required under generally accepted accounting principles. Therefore, the receiving division is a business activity meeting the definition of a component under AU-C section 600. All other information required to be included in the financial statements is prepared by the accounting and financial reporting function, which constitutes a business activity meeting the definition of a component under AU-C section 600.

The regional sales offices provide order information to the shipping division at the central distribution center and, therefore, do not provide any information that is required to be included in the financial statements by the financial reporting framework. For that reason, they would not be considered a business activity that meets the definition of a *component*.

Similarly, the purchasing and shipping divisions (discussed in the following paragraph) at the central distribution center do not provide any information that is required to be included in the financial statements. The purchasing division provides information to the receiving division related only to items ordered. Although purchase orders represent a commitment, they do not result in information that is included in the financial statements; therefore, the purchasing division does not meet the definition of a *business activity* that would be considered a component under AU-C section 600.

Sales and accounts receivable information is required to be included in the financial statements, but that information is prepared by the accounting department. This information is developed from pricing information maintained by the executive offices and shipping information maintained by the shipping division. Therefore, neither the executive office nor shipping division meets the definition of a *business activity* that would be considered a component under AU-C section 600. However, the group engagement team would likely consider these business activities using a "top down" risk assessment process.

A component auditor may be part of the group engagement partner's firm; the CPA firm's Arkansas office is a component auditor because it is performing work on financial information of a component (that is, inventory observation, risk assessment procedures for the central distribution center, and tests of controls over certain processes at the receiving division of the central distribution) that is included in the group financial statements (company financial statements). AU-C section 600 requires the group engagement team to determine the type of work to be performed by component auditors on its behalf and the nature, timing, and extent of its involvement in the work of component auditors. The engagement team will meet this requirement by, as noted in the facts, developing the audit plan and coordinating and overseeing the work performed by the Arkansas office of the CPA firm. The Georgia office does not meet the definition of a *component auditor* because it is not performing work on the financial information of a component; however, because the engagement team is requesting that the work be performed on its behalf, it is appropriate for the engagement team to develop the audit plan and coordinate and oversee the work performed by the Georgia office of the CPA firm.

Example 3—Private Sector Entity With One Location and One Auditor, Using Network Firm

Facts

This example uses most of the same facts as those in example 2 of this appendix, except as follows:

- The CPA firm has only one office, and it is located in California.

- The CPA firm will be using two network firms, one in Arkansas (Arkansas Firm) and one in Georgia (Georgia Firm), to assist in the financial statements audits.

Commentary

The fact that the other auditors assisting the engagement team are not from the same firm but from network firms does not change the engagement team's responsibilities or required procedures from those in the previous example. Arkansas Firm is a component auditor for the same reasons the Arkansas Office was in the previous example. Because the components on which Arkansas Firm will be performing audit procedures do not issue separate financial statements on which Arkansas Firm will be issuing an auditor's report, CPA Firm cannot make reference to the report of Arkansas Firm.

The Georgia office does not meet the definition of a *component auditor* because it is not performing work on the financial information of a component; however, because the engagement team is requesting that the work be performed on its behalf, it is appropriate for the engagement team to develop the audit plan and coordinate and oversee the work performed by the Georgia office of the CPA firm.

.176

Appendix D—Applying Group Materiality to Components

Example 1—Not-for-Profit Organization

CPA Firm will be auditing a nonprofit entity consisting of a national office and separate chapters located across the country. The following chart provides the chapter and consolidated balance sheets of the entity. This example assumes the group engagement team considered group materiality of $728,000 and group performance materiality of $546,000, as well as the following factors, when identifying the following significant components:

- Components that are separate legal entities and significant based on their individual financial significance to the group, for example, in the following table, National/Corporate, the New York chapter, and the Chicago chapter (indicated by double border)
- Components that are business activities and significant based on their individual financial significance to the group, for example, in the following table, the shared service centers (indicated by double border; accounts highlighted in gray are those whose transactions are processed by the shared service centers)
- Components that are significant components based on the existence of significant risks, for example, in the following table, investments for the Los Angeles chapter and other chapters (indicated by a single border)

The auditor of the group financial statements will reference the work of the component auditors auditing the Chicago chapter. The group engagement team will perform, or ask component auditors to perform on its behalf, procedures on selected financial information, including contributions receivable, investments, and accrued payroll (highlighted in gray), for the National/Corporate, shared service centers, New York chapter, Los Angeles chapter, and other chapters. No reference will be made to the component auditors performing these procedures.

	National/ Corporate	Shared Service Centers Contributions, Investments & Payroll	New York Chapter	Chicago Chapter	Los Angeles Chapter	Other Chapters	Total
Assets:							
Cash and cash equivalents	$662,958		$1,988,873	$1,104,929	$(65,953)	$728,911	$4,419,717
Contributions receivable	245,000	845,724	490,826	272,681	2,915	79,302	1,090,724
Investments	3,232,987	18,320,258	9,698,960	5,388,311	1,730,256	1,502,731	21,553,245
Beneficial interests in trusts	5,305,320		—		—	—	5,305,320
Land, building, and equipment, net	462,224		1,386,671	770,373	320,150	142,074	3,081,491
Other assets	142,438		427,313	237,396	60,214	82,224	949,585
Total assets	10,050,926		13,992,643	7,773,691	2,047,582	2,535,241	36,400,082
Liabilities:							
Accounts payable	$195,812		$587,436	$326,354	$64,259	$131,553	$1,305,414
Accrued payroll	349,414	1,980,014	1,048,243	582,357	164,329	185,085	2,329,428
Other accrued expenses	52,237		156,712	87,062	31,947	20,290	348,249
Deferred revenue	50,275		150,825	83,792	270	50,005	335,166
Other liabilities	561		1,683	935	—	561	3,739
Total liabilities	648,299		1,944,898	1,080,499	260,805	387,494	4,321,996
Net assets	9,402,626		12,047,745	6,693,192	1,786,777	2,147,747	32,078,086
Total liabilities and net assets	$10,050,926		$13,992,643	$7,773,691	$2,047,582	$2,535,241	$36,400,082

Applying Component Materiality

Some of the key considerations for the group when applying component materiality are as follows:

1. The group auditor will be referencing the work of the component auditor of the Chicago chapter. Therefore, there is no need to communicate component materiality to that auditor. However, the group auditor is required to consider all components when determining component materiality.

2. The group auditor intends to assume responsibility for the work of component auditors on the Los Angeles chapter and other chapters. Therefore, the group auditor is required to communicate the materiality to be used in performing procedures on the highlighted accounts. It is likely in this case, because the balances are small compared to the financial statement total amounts, that the group auditor will actually determine the scope of procedures to be performed based on the remaining available materiality.

3. The component auditors to be referred to will be auditing approximately 21 percent of total assets and 21 percent of net assets. As such, the group auditor may consider one-fifth of the $728,000 in group materiality to be applied to those components. The group auditor might estimate that component materiality of 75 percent to 85 percent of group materiality might be appropriate for the remaining components.

4. The group auditor may also consider, due to specific risks in the remaining components, to use a lesser level of materiality.

5. The combined component materiality may exceed group materiality as long as each component materiality is less than group materiality.

6. In addition, the group auditor is required to determine performance materiality for the remaining components.

Example 2—Multinational Manufacturing Company

This example is derived from the December 2008 issue of the *Journal of Accountancy* article "Component Materiality for Group Audits."[1] The example describes a large manufacturing company with 5 significant components operating in various jurisdictions around the world. The entity has the following revenue information for the significant components, which represents 90 percent of total revenue.

Component	Revenues
1	60,000,000
2	50,000,000
3	40,000,000
4	30,000,000
5	20,000,000
Total revenue	200,000,000

---

[1] The article and complete example can be found at www.journalofaccountancy.com/Issues/2008/Dec/ComponentMaterialityforGroupAudits.htm.

Using a benchmark of revenue, the group auditor has determined group materiality to be $1,000,000. Component materiality may be allocated as follows.

This table shows the proportionate allocation approach based on relative sales values.

Component	Revenue	Component Materiality
1	60,000,000	300,000
2	50,000,000	250,000
3	40,000,000	200,000
4	30,000,000	150,000
5	20,000,000	100,000
Total revenue	200,000,000	1,000,000

Alternatively, component materiality could be allocated to each component at an amount slightly below group materiality.

Component	Revenue	Component Materiality
1	60,000,000	900,000
2	50,000,000	900,000
3	40,000,000	900,000
4	30,000,000	900,000
5	20,000,000	900,000
Total revenue	200,000,000	4,500,000

Although both methods are permitted by AU-C section 600, *Special Considerations—Audits of Group Financial Statements (Including the Work of Component Auditors)* (AICPA, *Professional Standards*), the first is likely to be overly conservative and lead to too much audit work, and the second is likely to be too aggressive and increase the detection risk of a misstatement at the group level to an undesirably high level.

The Probabilistic Model

This method as described in the article uses a probabilistic model to increase the group materiality to a maximum aggregate group materiality based on the number of components. In this case, the factor used is 2.5 times. As such, the aggregate of component materiality is targeted at $2,500,000.

Once the aggregate is determined, there are two approaches to apply to the components. One is the straight relative revenue model as seen in the preceding table. The second is a weighted average method, using a sum of the squares approach. The following table illustrates the two approaches.

Component	Revenue	Proportionate Allocation	Weighted Average Allocation
1	60,000,000	750,000	622,750
2	50,000,000	625,000	568,500
3	40,000,000	500,000	508,600
4	30,000,000	375,000	440,600
5	20,000,000	250,000	359,550
Total revenue	200,000,000	2,500,000	2,500,000

The group auditor can then review this table and determine based on risk factors in specific components the final allocation of group materiality. This might look as follows.

Component	Revenue	Proportionate Allocation	Weighted Average Allocation	Group Engagement Team Determination
1	60,000,000	750,000	622,750	690,000
2	50,000,000	625,000	568,500	590,000
3	40,000,000	500,000	508,600	500,000
4	30,000,000	375,000	440,600	420,000
5	20,000,000	250,000	359,550	300,000
Total revenue	200,000,000	2,500,000	2,500,000	2,500,000

In all cases, the group auditor is required to consider specific risks and design an audit strategy that will effectively lower that risk to an acceptable level.

One should note that the preceding methodologies are neutral with respect to the role of component auditors. In situations in which the group auditor will be making reference to the work of the component auditor, it is still necessary to consider materiality even though it is not required to be communicated. If the group auditor can determine the materiality used by the component auditor, that may enable the group auditor to apply more materiality to other components.

For instance, if component five in the preceding example is to be audited by a component auditor and the group auditor is making reference, and if the component auditor intends to use $100,000 as materiality for that component, the group auditor has more aggregate materiality to apply to any or all of the other four components.

If the group auditor intends to take responsibility for the work of the component auditors and the required procedures are less than an audit adapted as necessary (that is, a review or procedures on certain accounts), the group auditor may want to reduce the materiality for those components and once again apply more component materiality to other components while retaining the same total aggregate component materiality.

Successfully applying component materiality can have many permutations and does not lend itself well to a formulaic approach. Proper planning and judgment are necessary in order to have an efficient and effective group audit.

.177

Appendix E—Additional Internet Resources

Here are some useful websites that may provide valuable information to accountants.

Website Name	Content	Website
AICPA	Summaries of recent auditing and other professional standards, as well as other AICPA activities.	www.aicpa.org www.cpa2biz.com www.ifrs.com
AICPA Financial Reporting Executive Committee	Summaries of recently issued guides, technical questions and answers, and practice bulletins containing financial, accounting, and reporting recommendations, among other things.	www.aicpa.org/FRC
AICPA Accounting and Review Services Committee	Summaries of review and compilation standards and interpretations.	www.aicpa.org/ RESEARCH/ STANDARDS/ COMPILATIONREVIEW/ ARSC/ Pages/ARSC .aspx
Economy.com	Source for analyses, data, forecasts, and information on the U.S. and world economies.	www.economy.com
The Federal Reserve Board	Source of key interest rates.	www.federalreserve.gov
Financial Accounting Standards Board (FASB)	Summaries of recent accounting pronouncements and other FASB activities.	www.fasb.org
Governmental Accountability Office (GAO)	*Government Auditing Standards* and other GAO activities.	www.gao.gov
Governmental Accounting Standards Board (GASB)	Summaries of recent accounting pronouncements and other GASB activities.	www.gasb.org

(continued)

Website Name	Content	Website
International Accounting Standards Board	Summaries of International Financial Reporting Standards and International Accounting Standards.	www.iasb.org
International Auditing and Assurance Standards Board	Summaries of International Standards on Auditing.	www.iaasb.org
International Federation of Accountants	Information on standards setting activities in the international arena.	www.ifac.org
Private Company Financial Reporting Committee	Information on the initiative to further improve FASB's standard setting process to consider needs of private companies and their constituents of financial reporting.	www.pcfr.org
Public Company Accounting Oversight Board (PCAOB)	Information on accounting and auditing activities of the PCAOB and other matters.	www.pcaob.org
Securities and Exchange Commission (SEC)	Information on current SEC rulemaking and the Electronic Data Gathering, Analysis, and Retrieval database.	www.sec.gov
USA.gov	Portal through which all government agencies can be accessed.	www.usa.gov

Printed in the United States
By Bookmasters